ACKNOWLEDGMENTS

 **W9-CDC-312**

We would like to thank Helen Albert and Cherilyn DeVries, our editors at Taunton, for their diligence in seeing this project through to completion. We would also like to thank Laurel Hendrix for her work on the preliminary drawings, and Rosemary Erickson and Magda Gilewicz for their belief in the book.

CONTENTS

Reliable Rain

A Practical Guide to Landscape Irrigation

Howard Hendrix and Stuart Straw

The Taunton Press

Cover photo: Mike Chen

Taunton
BOOKS & VIDEOS

for fellow enthusiasts

Text © 1998 by Howard Hendrix
Photos and illustrations © 1998 by The Taunton Press, Inc.

Printed in the United States of America
10 9 8 7 6 5 4 3 2 1

The Taunton Press, Inc., 63 South Main Street,
PO Box 5506, Newtown, CT 06470-5506
e-mail: tp@taunton.com

Library of Congress Cataloging-in-Publication Data

Hendrix, Howard V., 1959-
        Reliable rain : a practical guide to landscape irrigation / Howard V. Hendrix
and Stuart E. Straw.
              p.   cm.
        Includes index.
        ISBN 1-56158-202-6
        1. Landscape irrigation. I. Straw, Stuart E. II. Title
        SB475.82.H45   1997
        635'.0487—dc21   97-28744
                                                                CIP

INTRODUCTION

Gardening is all of a piece. You can't really pull out one aspect and talk about it in isolation. Even something as simple as mulching flower beds can't be discussed without considering the effect of mulch on weed germination and water retention. That's why, in this book about irrigation, we will be discussing not only watering but also types of soils, plants, climates—and much more.

The need for books like this one becomes particularly great when a field is undergoing rapid or revolutionary change, as landscape irrigation is today. Plant irrigation may be as old as civilization but it's also as new as the latest computer chip. High-tech approaches such as tensiometers and responsive computer control are still down the line yet for most of us, but there are many aspects of the "new irrigation" that are already applicable to the flower bed, vegetable patch, cottage garden, residential yard, and small orchard.

The techniques and approaches described in this book may be new and different, but they address the same old problem. Whether we're farmers, orchardists, or gardeners, we all want more orderly moisture than the chaotic weather system provides.

Through the hydrological cycle of moisture falling to the earth from the sky as rain, dew, or fog, and rising back to the sky as vapor, water plays a crucial role in that planetary heat-exchange engine we call the weather. Recent research indicates that the primary effect of the "greenhouse warming" of our planet will be upon the hydrological cycle. Weather will become even more unpredictable—a possibility that should give pause to any gardener or grower.

We can say not only that "the weather is changing" but also that "The weather is changing in its rate of change." Global weather patterns are increasingly unstable and may be characterized by more frequent and ferocious cyclonic storms such as tornadoes, hurricanes, and monsoons. Of equal importance to the gardener and grower is the other end of the pattern—the drought that alternates with the flood.

This is where "reliable rain" enters the picture. Irrigation can help to dampen the effects of the wilder fluctuations of the chaotic weather system, and artfully extend the rainy season through the dry parts of the year, so that we can grow the plants we wish to grow.

The first purpose of this book is to explain the "why" of irrigation and bring the garden enthusiast and small farmer up to speed on the current state of practical and affordable landscape irrigation. Whether you work the soil in an area where an irrigation system is a necessity, or in a region where an irrigation system is primarily a handy backup to the usual rainfall, we will provide you with efficient and convenient alternatives—both to watching plants shrivel and die and to lugging cumbersome hoses and sprinklers around.

Our second purpose is "how to." If you decide to put in an irrigation system, this book will show you how to do it yourself. When you have finished reading this book and working through its steps, you will have all the knowledge you'll need to be your own irrigation designer and installer.

This book includes an overview of the history of irrigation and a description of the current state of the art; a guide that will help you determine what type of irrigation system, if any, might be appropriate for your yard and garden; and step-by-step explanations of how to custom-design your own irrigation system, from the water main to the sprinkler head or emitter in the farthest corner of your property. We've also provided 10 fully illustrated descriptions of yard and garden irrigation designs. Finally, a glossary provides definitions of any specialized terms you may encounter.

Books like this one try to bridge the gap between the irrigation expert and the gardening enthusiast. We have emulated that bridge in the writing of this book. One of us (Stuart Straw) is an irrigation expert; the other (Howard Hendrix) is a novelist and teacher. Both of us are long-time gardening enthusiasts.

By applying what you read here, you will create a lusher yard and garden while saving time, money, and water. So read on—and happy watering!

CHAPTER 1

Efficient Watering Systems: Now More than Ever

Why put in an irrigation system? Most people would say, "To keep my plants healthy." Others might add, "To save time, money, and energy." Yet a watering system offers another important benefit. It frees up our time, so we can interact with our gardens at a higher level. Instead of dragging around hoses and buckets, we can spend time pruning, deadheading, harvesting—even mowing.

As most gardeners know, the difference between a landscape that's great and one that is merely okay has a lot to do with how much time the gardener gives to that landscape. A lawn or garden is not furniture; you can't just put it in place and forget about it, or the beauty of the living landscape will deteriorate.

Most of us today lead increasingly urbanized and clock-bound lives, which tend to alienate us from natural cycles and from the land on which we live. By reconnecting our personal time and space to that of the natural world around us, we take a big step forward from the model of "dominion over the earth" in the first chapter of Genesis to the model of stewardship found in the second chapter. And that's an appropriate place to start when telling the story of irrigation.

From the Flood to the Microspray

Adam and Eve were gardeners rather than farmers. Small-scale gardening, initially for sacred purposes, probably predates large-scale agriculture for food production. The great cradles of civilization—Egypt, Mesopotamia, India, China—were all built upon inundation agriculture, or irrigation by flooding. Not coincidentally, these lands were also the first great centers of the written word. That ancient knowledge can help us make more efficient use of today's water.

Over 5,000 years, the direction of irrigation has moved from the "macro" to the "micro"— from large-scale flooding to spot water application. This is particularly true in the last 50 years. You might say that irrigation has been working its way back to the garden.

CANAL WORK

Normally, water volumes increase as water moves downhill: Drops join to form trickles, trickles merge into rivulets, rivulets become streams, and streams turn into rivers. Traditional canal and channel work uses gravity in the other direction: Canals are split off into channels, which can then be split into furrows.

For most of history, irrigation has involved canals (see the photo below), channels, and some degree of flooding. Flood

The Friant-Kern Canal in California's Central Valley helps sustain one of the world's most productive agricultural regions.

Flood Irrigation Types

Basin Irrigation

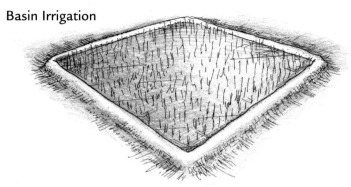

In basin irrigation, the entire area is flooded and surrounded by a dike.

Border Irrigation

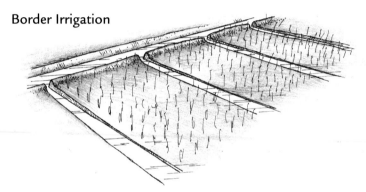

With the border irrigation method, water flows in from one side, passes through channels, and drains out the opposite side.

Furrow Irrigation

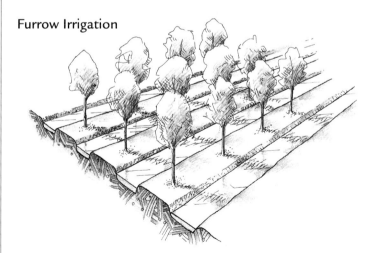

Furrow irrigation is the most efficient flooding method—water is channeled and confined.

irrigation falls into three types: basin, border, and furrow (see the drawing on the facing page).

Basin irrigation

In basin irrigation, the growing area must be more or less flat and surrounded by a dike to prevent runoff. This method works best where the soils are fairly slow in their uptake of water and the crops under cultivation are deep-rooted, planted close together, and tolerant of inundation. Rice paddies are the classic example of basin irrigation.

Basin irrigation encourages soil crusting and dust, and it requires higher dikes than other surface irrigation systems. In terms of water efficiency, this irrigation method is a gross waster. Less than half of the applied water is available for use by the crop. The rest is lost to runoff and evaporation.

Border irrigation

In this approach, the growing area is usually longer than it is wide and tends to have a bit of slope. There is no dike at the far end of the plot, as in basin irrigation. The flooding tends to be more controlled—small channels are generally dug from a larger main canal—but the water losses from gravity and evaporation are significant, about the same as in basin irrigation.

Furrow irrigation

This method tends to be more efficient than basin or border irrigation because the entire surface of the growing area is not inundated. The water is channeled into numerous small furrows or ditches, also called "creases" or "corrugations." This places the water somewhat more accurately, as water spreads both vertically and horizontally from the ditches into the sola, or soil body. Water flow can be controlled from furrow to furrow, so there is less waste and evaporation loss. Between 55% and 70% of the applied water is available for use by the crop.

Furrow irrigation can be made even more efficient through the use of an alternate-row strategy: Even-numbered rows are watered only on even-numbered days, and odd rows are watered only on odd days. Alternate-row strategies reduce the time, labor, and water costs of irrigating, with only a marginal reduction in crop yield per acre.

Difficulties associated with furrow irrigation include the loss of "tail water" (water that flows out the end of the furrow), the expense of developing the furrows, and the increase in potential erosion. Also, furrows are difficult to automate because the soil surface is constantly being plowed up; any permanent irrigation structure will be disturbed.

PIPE DREAMS

The furrow is about as far as such traditional methods can go in refining the flow of water. We need pipe to create the artificial trickles and rain drops necessary for yards, gardens, and small orchards. Irrigation methods that utilize pipe systems include sprinklers, Low-Energy Precision Application (LEPA), and trickle, or "drip," irrigation.

At their best, sprinklers simulate slow rainfall and thereby make it possible to irrigate not only flat, loamy surfaces but also irregular and sandy surfaces. Except in high-wind areas, sprinklers produce a more even application of water than most other methods. Because they don't require surface ditches and can be easily automated, sprinklers reduce the need for physical labor and make the growing area more accessible for machinery.

Sprinkler systems are either mobile or stationary; both varieties are available for the home garden space. As you might guess, their forebears were developed for large-scale agricultural use.

Mobile sprinkler systems

Large-scale mobile sprinkler setups are usually either center-pivot or lateral-move line systems. Both involve a pipeline suspended above a field, and both are usually self-propelled. The center-pivot system utilizes a swing-arm pipeline that is anchored to an upright at the center of the growing space. Center-pivot systems are responsible for the green circles amid brown desert that airline passengers often see when flying over arid zones of the American West.

A 90° microspray head in action. These units are great for tight corners, such as where the yard meets the house or driveway.

Those circular shapes dramatically illustrate a drawback to the center-pivot system: It can only irrigate a round area, and most land plots are square or rectangular. Some work has been done to help irrigate the square corner areas in these "crop circle" plots, but it remains an inherent difficulty of these systems. Center pivots can be adapted for both high- and low-pressure irrigation systems, however, and they apply water at fairly efficient rates—70% to 85%

is available to the crop (see the chart on p. 10 for more on this).

Lateral-move sprinkler systems are another landmark of the arid West: large-diameter wheels spaced at intervals along a central pipe axle (see the photos below). An engine mounted to this contraption propels the system slowly across the field. Lateral-move systems deliver water at an efficiency rate of 65% to 80%.

A large, overhead, self-propelled lateral-move sprinkler system in a field near Fresno, California.

This is an individual sprinkler unit on the lateral-move sprinkler system shown at left. Center-pivot systems use the same powerful heads.

Watering Efficiency by Delivery System

DELIVERY SYSTEM	WATERING EFFICIENCY
Mobile systems	
• center pivot sprinklers	70%-85%
• lateral-move line sprinklers	65%-80%
Stationary systems	
• fixed-head lawn sprinklers	65%-80%
• water guns	50%-65%
Low-Energy Precision Application (LEPA) systems	80%-90%
Trickle or drip systems	almost 100%

Low-Energy Precision Application
LEPA, as it is known, utilizes the center-pivot system, but instead of supplying water from over-head, it waters beneath the canopy leaves of the crop, almost directly to the roots, using long vertical pipe or dangling hose units. This limits the amount of water lost to evaporation and wind, and ensures a more even application. This type of system typically delivers 80% to 90% of applied water in a plant-usable form.

Stationary sprinkler systems
As their name implies, these sprinkler heads are fixed in place. Fixed-head lawn sprinklers are a common example, though much larger agricultural variants predate them. The efficiency of these systems ranges from 65% to 80%. Agricultural "big gun" or "water gun" systems have large orifices to help prevent clogging and can throw water in an arc up to 620 ft. in radius, reducing the number of units needed to irrigate a large space. They are 50% to 65% efficient in their water distribution.

Water losses in such stationary systems can be attributed to gravity, wind lofting (see p. 31), and evaporation. Other disadvantages are their initial cost and the fact that they occasionally clog with particulate matter.

Trickle and drip systems
Usually permanently mounted, these spot-flooding systems deliver almost 100% of applied water directly to the base of a plant, virtually eliminating losses due to wind and evaporation.

They also deliver water very slowly and precisely so that little, if any, is lost to runoff. Although these systems can deliver usable water to plants with tremendous efficiency, they do tend to clog from particulates in the water. Also, they can make harvesting a problem, since they are often permanently installed and you're forced to harvest around them. Trickle and drip systems present problems if you have to harvest by mowing. If you harvest by picking, however, this approach can work well. It has been used very successfully in orchards.

BACK TO THE GARDEN

Over the last 50 years, advances in agricultural irrigation have begun to spin off technologies into the world of landscaping. By fostering increasingly accurate control and placement of water, new technologies have become very important to yard and garden design, particularly in the drier climates of the Sunbelt and Southwest. However, droughts happen even in the Midwest and East, and serious gardeners in those regions have also begun to install irrigation systems as a back-up to "God water."

Before you design your own system for "reliable rain," take a moment to consider three important aspects of any landscape irrigation system: invisibility, pressure and flow, and timing.

Invisible irrigation

A key point to remember is that irrigation of any type functions as an infrastructural element for ensuring the health of your growing area. Unlike the situation in agricultural applications, your landscape watering system should be as close to invisible as you can make it, at least when it is not in operation. When the system is "on," it may have a certain aesthetic as well as functional value—multiple-stream rotor heads, for instance, have their own particular beauty when they are in operation (see the photo below). Generally, though, you want to call attention to your healthy plants, not to your irrigation system.

A multi-stream gear-driven head in action. Water-efficient and aesthetically pleasing, these heads are finding increasing use in the residential market.

This invisibility should be true in other aspects of your irrigation design as well. Your system should be designed so that it does not waste water by throwing or splashing it onto building walls or concrete walks. Wet concrete is slippery (think liability and lawsuits) and eventually breaks down (think expensive erosion repairs). Water on building walls can result in rot and the invasion of pests such as termites; allowing irrigation arcs to sweep over wooden fences not only encourages rot but also makes for aesthetically unpleasant water stains.

The effect of your watering on the soil should be nearly invisible as well. You should avoid creating moving water on the soil surface. Moving water makes for erosion. Pooled water at the surface should also be avoided—it evaporates more readily, decreasing the efficiency of your watering.

Pressure and flow

In landscape irrigation, we strive to apply water in a way that maximizes the match between the amount of water applied to a growing area and the field capacity of that area. Field capacity is a soil's capacity for holding water. It is this "held" water that is available for use by the plant. When this capacity is exceeded, gravity takes its toll in the form of runoff. We want to avoid runoff because it contributes to the silting up of streams, to groundwater pollu-

tion by nitrates, and to eutrophication (massive "blooms" and oxygen-depriving die-offs of algae, resulting from the flow of fertilizers into lakes).

Field capacity and runoff lead us to two other important physical parameters of water: pressure and flow. Pressure is the amount of force applied over a surface—in this context, usually described in pounds per square inch (psi). Flow is the quantity of water that moves past a given point over a given period of time—in this context, usually measured in gallons per minute (gpm). A fire hose and a woodland stream might have exactly the same flow rate, but very different pressures. You could stand in the stream with little difficulty, while the same flow rate coming out of a high-pressure fire hose might well blast you off your feet.

Generally, what we try to emulate in landscape irrigation is "gentle rain," which means low pressures and slow flow rates. "Low and slow" are key to avoiding pooling and runoff; they allow more time for the water to infiltrate or percolate into the soil body. A slower flow rate means that runoff is less, uptake is greater, and the ratio of applied water to field capacity more closely approaches the 1:1 ideal.

About all that can be said for fast rain and "volume dump" spraying is that, well, at least it's water! Irrigation that emulates a torrential downpour is inefficient. High flow rate means high runoff, mass wasting of both soil and water at the surface, and a poor ratio of applied water to field capacity.

Timing

Advancements in irrigation throughout this century have focused on putting usable water *where* it's needed—the spatial dimension. Increasingly, though, the future of irrigation will bring refinements in the temporal dimension—getting water to the plant *when* it's needed. This is called "irrigation scheduling," and we've already discussed a rudimentary form of it in the context of alternate-row furrow irrigation. Automated sprinkler controllers and control valves allow greater control over this time dimension, and they have become an integral part of any irrigation system for the yard, garden, or small orchard (see p. 26 and pp. 114-118).

The Irrigation Revolution

In many ways, the irrigation revolution in landscaping involves spinning off large-scale technologies originally developed for farms and golf courses, and applying them in smaller-scale uses. The categories of water delivery systems we discuss here reflect that refinement in scale. We can divide delivery systems into four categories that are based on how far a given type of sprinkler head throws water (see the chart below).

Sprinkler Throw Distances by Type

DELIVERY SYSTEM	OPTIMUM THROW DISTANCE
Macro Water guns, impact heads, single-stream rotors	greater than 30 ft.
Meso Stream rotors with shorter throw arcs	8 ft.-30 ft.
Micro Plastic spray angles on risers	2 ft.-10 ft.
Bubbler or soaker Shrubblers, drip lines, soaker hose lines	spot or linear watering, micro flooding at base of plant

This "Shrubbler" unit is intermediate in throw between microspray and a dripper, usually providing 1 ft. or less of throw.

The same goes for bubblers: As there's some overlap between microspray, drip, and soaker line, we will categorize them all as micro systems in the discussion that follows. The key thing to remember is throw distance, which ranges from zero in the most precise micro systems to well over 30 ft. in the most powerful macro systems (see the chart on p. 13).

The primary determining factors for deciding whether to use micro or macro systems in a given area are costs (measured in both money and labor), the type of vegetation or crop, the distribution of that vegetation, and water efficiency.

Macro systems generally have an optimum throw-arc or pattern of more than 30 ft. from the sprinkler head to the point at which the farthest droplets fall to earth. Meso systems throw best between 8 ft. and 30 ft. Micro systems throw between 2 ft. and 10 ft. Bubbler or soaker systems are essentially spot or linear watering, microflooding of a particularly limited location, usually at the base of a plant (see the photo above).

These gradations are rules of thumb and not absolutes. Water guns, impact heads, and single-stream rotors are all macro systems, though some stream rotors qualify in the meso category because of their shorter optimum throw arc. For that reason we will, for discussion purposes, include meso units under the general macro category.

MACRO DELIVERY SYSTEMS

When we speak of macros, we're usually talking about water guns, impact-driven heads, multiple-stream rotors, and the larger flat-spray pop-ups. In general, macro systems emulate cumulo-nimbus clouds and the significant levels of rain they produce. Macros resemble big agricultural irrigation systems. The more the area to be irrigated resembles a farm field (flat, big, loamy, and square), the more appropriate a macro system will be.

Costs

Because of their higher pressure and flow rates per head, macros tend to self-flush easily and require less labor and maintenance than micro systems. Their greater throw distance means that although macro heads are more expensive per unit than micros, far fewer macro heads are required to cover a given area. A pop-up macro head may cost $5, far more than a 50-cent micro-spray head, but odds are that the pop-up will do the job of more than 10 microspray units.

Water efficiency

Efficiency of water use is hampered by the larger scale of macro units. Impact heads, the least high-tech of the macros discussed here, are good at putting big quantities of water on the ground, but they tend to throw the bulk of their water to the farther half of the throw pattern (see the photo at left below). Water guns and stream rotors are generally more efficient than impact-driven heads because their water droplets are dispersed more evenly throughout the throw pattern (see the photo at right below).

Crop

Macros do best on plantings that don't mind being pelted with water from overhead. Though that's the way rain works, the fact is that not all plants do well with such overhead watering. The impact of overhead water droplets on rose leaves tends to spread fungus throughout the plant's surfaces. Micro systems such as bubblers, soaker hose, and microspray heads are thus more appropriate for roses.

The impact-driven head is an older irrigation technology often used in large-scale applications.

A single-stream gear-driven head. Such "water gun" heads are increasingly replacing impact heads in large-scale applications.

Just the opposite is true for crops such as lawns. A grass lawn is very much like a monoculture farm field; mowing is a sort of preemptive harvesting. Macro heads are well-suited to grass lawn applications, while micro systems such as soaker hose and standing microspray units are not.

Pop-up heads are particularly appropriate for lawn applications. They are virtually invisible until the system comes on. When that happens, water pressure in the line causes the spray head to pop out of the buried body of the unit. As shown in the photo below, in a well-designed and properly installed system, the top of this unit is just at surface level, and the pop-up riser lifts the head above the level of grass or flowers (these risers range in size from 2 in. to 12 in.). When the system shuts off, the loss of pressure causes the riser to drop back down into the unit's buried body, where it is out of sight and below the level of a lawn mower's blades.

Pop-ups come in models ranging from stationary orifice sprays to stream rotors and similar gear-controlled heads, all the way up to single-stream rotor water guns. A rule of thumb worth remembering: The riser for your pop-up heads should be taller than your tallest grass blade or flower spike (see the photo at left).

Coverage

For macros in general, angles and clearances also figure prominently in the horizontal dimension. This horizontal angle, called sweep or coverage, defines how much of a circle's 360° is swept by the spray from a given head.

Spray heads offer all sorts of coverage patterns, the most common being 45°, 90°, 180°, 270°, and 360°. Some spray heads produce adjustable

A hybrid unit in action, featuring a pop-up riser retrofitted with a 90° microspray head.

coverage patterns, offering an entire spectrum of angles and degrees. Such flange- or dial-adjustable heads are ideal for making the most of your possibilities as your garden evolves over time.

Head-to-head spacing of spray heads generally provides the most efficient coverage of the area slated to be irrigated (see the top drawing at right). "Tight" areas can also be done in square spacing with flat heads, which have a low throw-angle (see the bottom drawing at right). In any case, space your spray heads to avoid "rain shadows" (unwatered areas) caused by plants or trees interrupting the spray pattern.

MICRO DELIVERY SYSTEMS

Micro systems include any number of microspray types, from spray heads of varying coverage angles on stationary risers to misters, "spiders," and bubblers, to the ultimate porosity of soaker hose. In all cases, micros emulate the long, slow drizzle of strato-nimbus clouds, and allow you to pinpoint specific areas of your landscape. Small or oddly shaped beds or shrub lines, garden patches woven into forested areas—these are best served by the precision of micro units.

Water efficiency

Micro systems are more water-efficient than macro systems, particularly in sloping areas or heavy clay soils, where their low pressure and slow flow rates are a

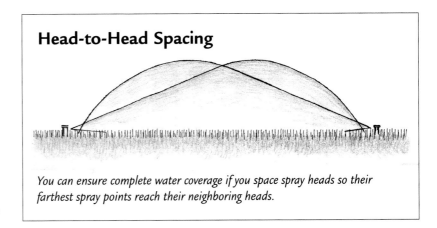

Head-to-Head Spacing

You can ensure complete water coverage if you space spray heads so their farthest spray points reach their neighboring heads.

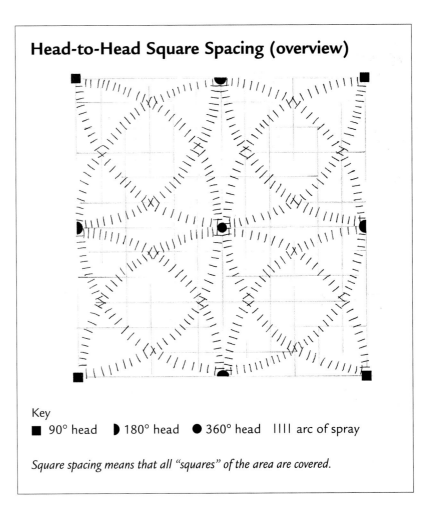

Head-to-Head Square Spacing (overview)

Key
■ 90° head   ◗ 180° head   ● 360° head |||| arc of spray

Square spacing means that all "squares" of the area are covered.

A standard microspray unit, showing the basic parts: spray head, riser, spike, and distribution line. The whitish hard-water deposits pose no problem, but they can be a nuisance inside the system if they clog the tiny spray head orifice inside.

distinct advantage. This low and slow aspect of microsystems is a cause of one of their basic drawbacks, however. Because their low flows move through very small apertures, micros do not generally flush themselves clean as readily as macro systems do. The result is that micro systems tend to clog with small particulates, especially in areas of hard water—and most of the piped water on this planet is hard. The photo at left shows the residue from hard water.

Costs

Micro delivery systems usually involve considerably less capital outlay at the start than macro systems. Micro heads are much less expensive per unit, but because they tend to clog, they are often more labor-intensive over the long run.

The single exception to this clogging problem is soaker hose, or soaker line. What we mean by soaker hose is not the green flat hose with little pinholes that you may recall from childhood summers. We're referring to black, spongy hose line, usually made from recycled tires, in which the entire tube is porous (see the photo below).

In many instances, soaker hose combines the low and slow virtues of micro systems, and their water efficiency, with the resistance to clogging characteristic of macro heads. Soaker hose has the added advantage of near invisibility—for instance, when it's fitted with a flow regulator and woven in at the bottom of a line of shrubs. You can also put top dressing over soaker hose, burying it without fear of clogging it.

Soaker hose works best in long, narrow spaces.

Because soaker hose has a pre-determined and largely unalterable number of "holes," some sort of pressure regulation is required if you don't want your soaker line to bob and weave like a tortured snake when your watering system is pumping. You can buy a flow or pressure regulator, or easily and cheaply make your own by laying a few washers—with water-restricting holes of various sizes—inside the female end of the soaker line (see the photo at right).

You can create a cheap and simple flow regulator for soaker hose by inserting washers in the female end.

Coverage

Like bubblers and drippers, soaker hoses are "microflooding" and work best in long, narrow spaces resembling the dimensions of the hose itself. A soaker hose has a throw of essentially zero; lateral spread depends upon the way in which the water from the soaker percolates or infiltrates through the soil body. Fogger and mister microspray heads have a similarly limited throw pattern and are largely dependent on wind currents for water dispersal.

Crops

Soaker hose is particularly appropriate for watering lines of shrubs and hedges, from rose bushes to grape holly to yews. It is also appropriate for narrow flower beds. It does not work well for large squares of lawn.

Bubblers are the best micro solution for hanging pots. Misters and foggers have more limited but interesting applications, working well for moss gardens, fern gardens, terrestrial orchids, and the like.

Pressure and flow

Micro heads tend to involve a "stepping down" of both pressure and flow from your hose bibb, main water line, or wellhead. The smaller the pipe you use, the more pressure and flow you lose, a result of the friction of water against the sides of the pipe. This stepping down will not pose a problem if you've got plenty of pressure and flow at your hose bibb, main household water line, or wellhead. If, however, you are beginning with low pressures and flows, you will need to take these factors into account, and may need to consider tank storage and pressurization.

You'll find a fuller discussion of pressures and flows on pp. 45-49, and information about tank storage and pressurization on pp. 62-63.

LANDSCAPE IRRIGATION HARDWARE

The discussion of pressures and pipe sizes inevitably leads to the fact that these days most irrigation pipe is plastic (see the photo below). Above and beyond the cost savings, the best reason for choosing plastic instead of metal is that it does not oxidize. Remember that galvanized pipe is only galvanized (zinc-coated) on the outside. Inside, it is just iron pipe, which oxidizes. Oxidized metal particles can clog your spray heads and oxidization can also create abrasive, high-friction zones throughout the pipe's length, restricting water flow.

If you are retrofitting an older irrigation system, therefore, we recommend that you replace as much as possible of the galvanized or copper pipe with polyvinyl chloride (PVC) plastic

These fittings will provide the transition from PVC to poly hose. From left to right: a threaded PVC elbow, a threaded-male-to-slip-PVC straight coupler, a black compression fitting, and ½-in. black poly hose.

pipe or polyethylene plastic hose, known as poly hose.

PVC

Pipe made from PVC is relatively cheap and won't break down in the soil the way galvanized or copper pipe will. Unlike copper, which has to be "lead sweated" (essentially a form of low-level welding), or galvanized (which can require a lot of heavy pipe-wrenching), lengths of PVC pipe are usually meshed together chemically by PVC cement. As a result, PVC below ground is much easier to maintain and repair than galvanized or copper pipe.

The downside of PVC manifests itself above ground. Although there are some expensive varieties of PVC that have been treated with ultraviolet protectants, most PVC tends to become brittle and warped after prolonged exposure to sunlight. Metal pipes don't have this weakness. The brittleness of PVC under even the best conditions gives metal another advantage, at least near the surface: Metal pipes have considerable tensile strength, and can better withstand the expansion of freezing water than PVC can. Freezing can break or burst PVC quite easily.

For these reasons, we recommend a hybrid system for your irrigation infrastructure: metal manifolds above ground and plastic pipe buried below, where

exposure to light and weather are minimized (see the photo below). This way you get the best of both worlds—tensile strength, and UV and freezing resistance above ground; inexpensiveness per foot, oxidization resistance, freer flow, and ease of repair below ground.

Polyethylene hose

You can hybridize your water delivery system even further with poly hose. Another plastic product, poly hose can be buried at a shallow depth or run across the soil surface—it's not UV-sensitive. It's also very flexible, and unlikely to warp or burst.

This six-valve, hybrid metal-plastic manifold allows us to exploit both metal's strength and rigidity, and plastic's flexibility and inexpensiveness.

You don't even have to glue poly hose (see the photo at left below). Compression fittings—slanted slip rings that you push the end of a length of poly hose into—work best. (You also can push the hose line over a type of connector called a slip barb, but this arrangement is not quite as resistant to slippage.)

Poly hose is a very appropriate delivery system for large flower beds and orchards. Though the surface lines are highly visible at first, they tend to disappear as plants grow in.

Poly hose is also a good springboard from which to work with "black spaghetti," the thin distribution lines most often used with microspray systems (see the photo at right below). (Microspray systems are discussed more fully on pp. 17-20 and shown in the photo on p. 18.) However, flexible poly hose should not be used in manifolds, which require rigid pipe to hold control valves in place.

CONTROL SYSTEMS

You can get away without installing clocks and timers if your irrigation system is fairly simple and you can count on yourself to turn it on and off. Memory often fails, however,

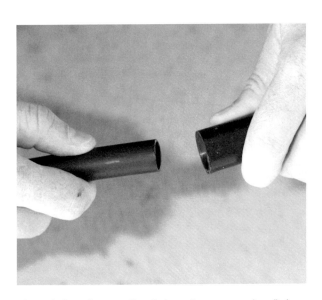

The poly hose inserts directly into the compression fitting, eliminating the need for glue.

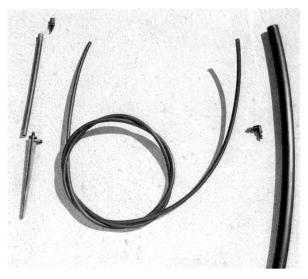

A basic assembly for microspray. From left to right: spray head, riser, spike, coiled ¼-in. "spaghetti" distribution line, elbow barb, and ½-in. poly hose.

and the more complex your irrigation system is, the more you're asking yourself to remember. Installing a timer may seem like a worry and an aggravation, but it will save you a good deal of both in the long term.

Control systems in landscape irrigation consist mainly of valves and switches that orient your water flow in terms of quantity—time, space, and pressure. The valves fall into two main groups: active and passive.

High-Tech Control Systems

A major advance in irrigation control has come about recently as growers—particularly wine-grape growers—have begun installing computer-automated moisture-monitoring devices. These systems measure soil moisture and climatic conditions and "decide" when to apply precise amounts of water during the crop's growth and reproductive cycles. This is truly high-tech watering.

Some of the newer technologies now coming on-line are a curious mix of active and passive control. A tensiometer, for instance, is essentially a "smart" valve controller. It is passive in that it contains a ceramic cone that allows water to flow back and forth into a column. Yet it also incorporates an apparatus that measures water in the column, which in turn measures the water content of the soil. Via this apparatus, the tensiometer's computer loop can activate the irrigation system and "schedule" irrigation without need of a sprinkler controller. A consid-

erable number of vineyards in northern California have successfully converted to tensiometer-driven irrigation systems. However, there are potential drawbacks, particularly for home use.

The tacit assumption behind a tensiometer is that the applied water will infiltrate into the soil in the appropriate manner for shutting down the system at the proper time. Unfortunately, soil is not always so cooperative. Pooling of water around the tensiometer may fool the system into believing that the plant is getting enough water when in fact the plant is parched, or the tensiometer may read the soil as drier than it actually is in the root zone, causing the roots to rot. And there's always the chance that the tensiometer will decide to water in the middle of your garden party.

Although tensiometers are still out of reach for the average gardener, we predict that in another decade these advanced controls will be refined and available for home landscaping

use. Given the recent history of irrigation, in which products and processes originally developed for large-scale agricultural and horticultural production have increasingly spun off into smaller-scale landscape use, it seems likely that the "smart home" of the near future will also incorporate a smart yard. Despite the occasional bumps and rough spots, the road to the future in irrigation, as elsewhere, appears to be an information highway.

Does all this technology mean humans will no longer play a part in irrigation and garden infrastructure? Hardly. Highly automated systems require humans to service them, at the very least, and the more complex the system, the greater its potential for breakdown. Paradoxically, automation sometimes drives the homeowner out of the role of gardener or small farmer and into the role of repairperson. For the foreseeable future, the landscape will likely remain an interactive place with a distinct need for human participation.

Passive control

Most irrigation systems make use of some passive control systems. The most common are purge valves and pressure regulators.

A purge valve (shown in the photo below) is a real boon if you are using plastic PVC pipe in cold climates. Purge valves (also referred to as drain plugs) allow water to drain out of a pipe when the water pressure falls below a pre-set value (usually about 5 psi). When you turn off the water flow to your irrigation system for the winter and the pressure in the pipes falls below 5 psi, the valve in the drain plug opens and any remaining water drains out of the pipes, making freeze-bursting far less likely.

Purge valves passively exploit two physical properties: gravity and water's cohesion. Water adheres to other surfaces, and coheres to itself. When a valve opens in a drain plug, the water drains not only from above the plug but also as far along the pipeline as gravity and adhesion will allow. To be on the safe side, we recommend installing a purge

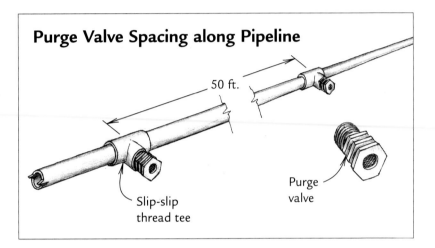

Purge Valve Spacing along Pipeline

50 ft.

Slip-slip
thread tee

Purge
valve

This is the assembly for a purge valve or "drain plug." These devices help protect irrigation pipes from bursting in freezing weather.

valve approximately every 50 ft. along the PVC pipe line (see the drawing on the facing page).

Pressure regulators (shown in the photo below) make use of the same properties as the purge valve, but to the opposite effect. They go into operation when the water pressure rises above a certain critical value. Pressure regulators are necessary when you have too much pressure, which can result in a condition known as "water hammer." Water hammer banging through your pipes can batter your sprinkler heads to pieces over time—or even cause your pipes to burst immediately.

As we mentioned earlier, some sort of pressure regulation is often necessary for soaker hose and drip lines. Overly high pressures can cause the water coming out of microspray heads to "fog": The water droplets' surface tension is overcome and they implode into a mist or fog. Some manufacturers take this problem into account at the spray head end, equipping their heads with anti-fogging devices. The same is true for bubblers, many designs of which now have a self-regulating pressure feature.

In-line water filter units and fertilizer injectors are also technically passive types of control, but they are more concerned with water quality than with water quantity.

Active control

Active or control valves usually depend not on gravity or water pressure for activation, but instead on an input signal. In manual systems, that signal occurs when someone physically opens the valve. In automated systems, the signal to open the valve is electrical and usually comes from a clock sprinkler controller (see the top photo on p. 26).

A sprinkler valve controller is essentially a clock timer that tells your irrigation system when,

In-line options for your system. From left to right: a water filter unit (disassembled, showing the screen filter), a pressure regulator unit (with sample pressure gauge, top), and a fertilizer injector (with hose to the fertilizer solution source).

This standard multistation timer incorporates both analog and digital elements and is housed in a waterproof box.

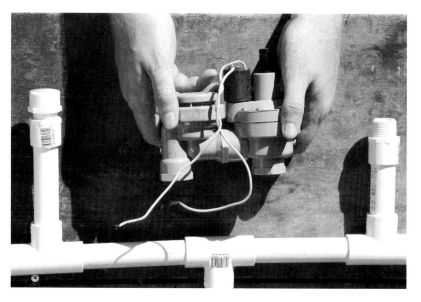

An automated control valve in plastic.

how long, and how often to water, as well as which pipelines and spray heads to use. The electrical current frees a current of water to flow through your pipes and out of your spray heads.

We'll have much more to say about control system design later. The key thing to remember here is, "Optimize your possibilities." It's true that control valves (shown in the photo below) cost money (between $10 and $30, depending on the size and material), but the point is not to use as few of them as possible. Instead, maximize the number of stations on your sprinkler controller.

If you think you'll need four stations, get a six-station controller. If you think you'll need six stations to cover your landscape's watering needs, get nine. Always purchase a sprinkler controller with at least two stations more than you initially think you'll need. We can almost guarantee that as your landscape develops you'll need those "extra" stations. You will save yourself time and frustration later by keeping your options open now.

Bear in mind that when you finally mount your sprinkler controller, you should be sure to position it where it will be readily accessible but not exposed to wet weather. We recommend housing it inside a waterproof box attached to your house or garage.

CHAPTER 2

Irrigation and Your Yard: Evaluating Your Needs

To determine the kind of irrigation that is appropriate for your landscape—or whether you should irrigate at all—you need to consider five important factors. What is the climate in your area, particularly the range of precipitation and temperature as recorded by the weather service and your local agricultural agent over the last 10 to 20 years? What's the major soil type in your landscape? What are the microclimates in your landscape? What are the types of plants involved and the history and probable future of your yard and garden? Once you've answered these questions, you'll be much better prepared to sit down and plan an irrigation system for your yard.

Climate

Climate involves not only precipitation, temperature, and air movement but also the types of moisture, heat, cold, and wind, and when they occur. A subfreezing night in late April is likely to do more above-ground damage to your growing plants and functioning irrigation system than a subfreezing night in early January, when both your plants and irrigation system are "asleep." The most important tool for learning about your climate is simple: observation.

PRECIPITATION

You need to determine how much precipitation your plants require and how much "God water" they are getting in the form of rain, snow, fog, and dew. You can find out quantitatively by putting up a rain gauge or watching the local weather on television. Getting a sense of your area's general precipitation patterns will help you determine the most critical time for irrigating. We can't tell you exactly how much water your plants will need, however. Your local cooperative extension agent can give you specific information about your area, but you also will have to spend some time walking around in and getting to know your own landscape.

In the inland areas of central and southern California, where we live, nearly all of our precipitation occurs between November and April. Our climate is very hot (100°F or more, often for weeks at a time) and pretty much bone-dry from May through October, especially in drought years. In much of the Southwest and Sunbelt, we have to stretch the ends of the rainy season to cover the summer as well.

Although conditions may not be as rigorous where you live, even the Midwest and East Coast have been known to experience seasonal droughts, and irrigation systems are important back-ups that can save your plantings. Irrigation provides "reliable rain" by controlling the amounts, types, and timing of moisture, and there are times when almost any homeowner, gardener, orchardist, or small farmer will benefit.

Remember that what we are striving for is the "slow rain" effect, to minimize runoff and increase uptake by plants (see p. 12). In general, we recommend watering more deeply and less often. Even in hotter, drier climates, you should avoid watering every day, if possible. Instead of watering from a given station 10 minutes every day, consider watering every other

An impact head provides long throws and large volumes of water. This type of head is appropriate for large monoculture growing areas, such as lawns or grain fields.

day or every third day for a longer period (half an hour, say) from spray heads that put out water at lower pressures and slower flow rates. Irrigation systems allow you to tailor the type of water you're putting down to the type of "crop" you're growing—from the thunderstorm or cloudburst-like watering from an impact head (shown in the photo on the facing page), to fine misters and foggers (shown in the photo at right).

If your plants seem unable to survive without daily watering, you should consider raising plants that are more drought-tolerant and appropriate to your climatic conditions (see pp. 36-37).

The only major exception to "low and slow" as the preferred approach is when you're growing your plants in sand with a high salt content. High flow rate can be valuable for flushing or "busting" the salt out of that soil. But there are less wasteful and damaging ways to get rid of that salt, including the application of gypsum to the soil.

TEMPERATURE

The effects of precipitation are thoroughly intertwined with temperature. Although it may seem strange to discuss the ways that heat and cold affect irrigation systems before we talk about how they affect plants, your plants and your irrigation are closely related.

A fogger in action. Here, droplet implosion is intentional; the cool mists benefit moss and rock gardens.

Low temperatures

The winter ice pressures that cause plant cells to rupture can also cause your irrigation pipes to burst. Subfreezing winter temperatures mean that drain plug purge valves will be a necessity (see p. 24). In such climates it's a good idea to bury your irrigation's infrastructure at least 6 in. below the depth to which the ground ordinarily freezes (see the photo below). You also should wrap insulation around the part of the gate valve that's above ground, if it carries water year-round.

Pipe in a trenchline at a 4,800-ft. elevation in the Sierra Nevada Mountains. The trenchline has been dug deeply to minimize the risk of frost damage.

Winter is hardly all bad, however. Snowmelt is "low and slow" moisture. Snow itself is actually a good thing for your cold-tolerant plants; when it snows there's a thin, insulating layer of water between the snow and the soil particles. The phrase "snow blankets the ground" is not only metaphorically but also quite literally true.

Cold, dry weather puts the most strain on plants—even more than hot and dry weather. The most rigorous climates on earth are cold deserts, which break plant chloroplasts and severely curtail the uptake of nutrients and water from the soil.

High temperatures

Warm, wet conditions such as those in a tropical rainforest are the best for plant growth. Even cool and wet is good: Consider the amount of plant material generated by the temperate rainforests of the Pacific Northwest.

The hot, dry summers found in many parts of North America present their own challenges. High temperatures mean we can't reap the benefit of morning dew, because the air doesn't get cool enough, even at night. Evaporation and evapotranspiration are factors for you and your plants to reckon with, particularly under the midday sun. (Evapotranspiration is the total loss of water from the soil, including that caused by evaporation and that caused by plant transpiration.)

If you're faced with dry heat, it helps to put more water out, particularly during spells of hot, windy weather. If summer heat is accompanied by high humidity, higher levels of watering won't help much because the humidity will keep the plant from transpiring or evaporating off its internal water efficiently. Don't go overboard on your watering. Instead, fertilize against summer stress with mineral products, particularly iron, potassium, and zinc in plant-usable forms.

The best times to water are around sunrise and/or around sunset. Watering during the heat of the day is bad because you'll lose excessive amounts of water to evaporation from both the air and the ground. The accepted rule of thumb is to water before 10 A.M. and after 4 P.M.—hours that also allow you to see your system in operation. This depends on your personal schedule, of course, but the closer to sunrise and/or sunset, the better.

AIR MOVEMENT

Wind can decrease the efficiency of an irrigation system, not only through evaporation and evapotranspiration, but also through lofting. In lofting, wind not only blows water out of its normal spray pattern, but also causes the water droplets to implode, turning a percentage of the water output into unintended mist or fog—tiny droplets that loft farther and evaporate more quickly.

Water droplets throw farthest when they are sprayed at a vertical angle of 45°, but they have least loft at a "flat" spray of 0°. Most spray heads have an optimum throw angle of approximately 22.5° to the vertical— an angle that maximizes throw while minimizing loft. A similar tug-of-war also exists in regard to droplet size. Most sprinkler manufacturers now design droplet size for maximal throw distance and minimal implosion.

It's possible to work with wind patterns. Here's where observation helps. If you know that summer evening breezes begin to pick up on your property at 6 P.M., you should water at 5 P.M. If you find that certain areas of your landscape are wind-whipped and the plants there tend to dry out and "burn," water those areas more deeply, during times when the air is calmer.

Soil Types

When evaluating your irrigation needs, the second major factor you need to consider is the type of soil you're growing your plants in. You want to get the best possible match between irrigation practices, field capacity (see p. 12), and plant uptake of applied water. How well a soil drains or retains water is primarily a function of the average size of the soil particles.

CLAY

Because of the small particles in clay soil, it takes longer for water to work its way into the soil body; once the water has worked its way in, it takes longer for the soil to dry out. This can be a good thing—you can keep clay soil damp with less irrigation.

You can improve a clay soil's texture, porosity, and tilth (how easily it breaks up), and thus its field capacity for water, by adding organic material, oyster shell, gypsum, or gypsite. The calcium in the latter three is particularly valuable because it acts as a nucleus, giving the clay particles something to adhere to and opening pores in the soil, improving water infiltration. Clay is a good mineral reserve, but it will tend to devour the organic material you dress it with, so repeated applications of organic matter are usually necessary. This is worth the effort; adding organic matter to clay tends to open up pore space physically, just as adding calcium does chemically.

Thick and solid, clay soil requires time to saturate with water and time to dry once it's wet.

Sandy loam soil is ideal for most gardening and growing needs.

LOAM

Loam, particularly sandy loam, is probably the best soil you could ask for. Goldilocks would love it: The particles are neither too big nor too small, but just right. Its water retention capacity is further aided by the presence of abundant organic material and soil micronutrients.

West of the Rockies, our soil is often characterized by micronutrient deficiencies. Of course, even in the Midwest and East, the best soils are often found in flood plains and river bottoms, which are hardly the best places for yards. So sandy loam is something of a limited resource.

SAND

This soil type is the opposite of clay: Water is "quick in, quick out," infiltrating rapidly but running through or evaporating out more quickly, as if the soil column were a jar full of marbles. Paradoxically, the same calcium-containing soil amendments that improve the tilth, texture, and porosity of clay—oyster shell, gypsum, and gypsite—also improve sandy soils. The calcium adheres to the soil particles, forming a matrix that slows water loss. The addition of these calcium-rich amendments also releases sulfur in the soil—a mild acidifying reaction that can be beneficial. Organic material can also be used to improve the water retention of sandy soil; the organic matter acts as a water reservoir.

You may wonder, "Well, if the particle size of sand is too big and the particle size of clay is too small, why not just add sand to clay and mix them together?" Although this can be effective in some limited, top-dressing contexts, we don't recommend it as a general procedure. If you mix the two soil types, you run the risk of combining the worst qualities of both. Concrete, you may recall, is primarily sand and clay.

Damp, sandy soil. Note the large particle size.

DECOMPOSED ROCK STRATA

In the West and Southwest, particularly in mountainous and alluvial fan areas, the decomposed rock strata most commonly encountered is decomposed granite. Because much of the West and Southwest is made up of mountain ranges and intermountain basins, this is a surprisingly common soil type in the region.

In granite, the dark minerals erode first, followed by the potassium. This means that although decomposed granite has a large overall matrix, it often contains a considerable range of particle sizes (see the photo below). The best way to improve the field capacity of these soils is to add organic matter, which can serve as either water reservoir or porosity enhancer, depending on the particle sizes.

SOIL pH

Generally, alkaline soils predominate nationwide. Ocean and desert environments tend to be alkaline, and that's where most sandy soils are found. The acidity found in some loamy and decomposed rock soils is largely a result of organic material incorporated into the soil body. Soil pH is adjustable and usually does not have a pronounced effect on field capacity.

Yard Microclimates

Before designing your irrigation system, you also should consider your yard's microclimates. You'll need to tailor your various irrigation stations to the amount of sunlight and wind each section of your landscape receives.

The north sides of houses, high hedges, and privacy fences, as well as areas beneath arbors and tree cover, tend to be cooler and shadier, and generally require less water. The hottest and driest areas of your landscape will generally be those with a southwest or bright afternoon exposure, without shade from trees or shadows from buildings. These areas will require more water.

As you gain shade through new yard structures or growing plants and trees, you will need to adjust your watering system

The water retention of decomposed granite soil is similar to that of sandy soil, though a bit less predictable because of the wide range of particle sizes in the decomposed rock.

accordingly. What you're ultimately after are fewer but deeper waterings, which will improve root growth and penetration. Root growth is a good corrective to runoff on steeper slopes and to pooling in flat areas. (Ground cover plantings and organic matter also serve to suck up excess water so it won't run off, or pool and evaporate.)

In general, you should water less on steeper slopes. You should strive for the "slow rain" effect, to improve the chances of water infiltration into the soil body and to avoid runoff. Soaker hose and microspray are both appropriate options for hillsides. On flat areas, higher-pressure and faster-flow systems such as water guns, big stream rotors, and impact-driven heads can be more readily tolerated.

Plants

If you are working with an existing landscape, you will most likely be trying to match your irrigation to the needs of your existing plantings. If you have not put in your landscape, or if you're planning a major retrofit, you may want to read this section with the future in mind: What type of plantings will you want, and how much water will they need?

We have slanted this chapter a bit toward new installation or retrofit of a landscape, but the descriptions apply both to the plants you already have and to the ones you are hoping to put in soon.

Beneficial Fungi

Healthy soil is an ecosystem with remarkable diversity and carrying capacity. Many plants in established environments have important partners in beneficial fungi, which help them gather water and nutrients.

The issue in landscaping is not only how much water penetrates and is held by the soil—it's also how thoroughly the plants' roots make use of that water. In the mycorrhizal relationship, as it's known, beneficial fungi on plant roots act as a network that makes more nourishment and moisture available to the host plant. The fungi essentially increase the surface area of the plant's root system.

Trees particularly benefit from their symbiotic association with beneficial fungi. Because the fungi work best when undisturbed, they tend to help perennial plants more than they do annuals.

Today you can buy mycorrhizal dips and other micro-level preplanting treatments designed to boost the efficiency of water uptake by your plants. Very new to the market, these products are helping to fine-tune the role of irrigation in landscaping (see Sources of Supply on p. 137 for the addresses of companies that supply these treatments).

WATER NEEDS

Because the plants found in yards, orchards, and farms developed in a variety of climates under diverse conditions, determining the water needs of a particular plant species is often a challenge. Tolerance to drought, like tolerance to flooding, is not so much a yes/no situation as it is a spectrum of adaptations by various plants to varied levels and schedulings of water. Plants generally can be divided into three categories: xeriscape, drought-tolerant, and drought-intolerant.

Xeriscape

Meaning "dry landscape" and implying zero or almost no watering, xeriscape has been a frequent buzzword for some years now. It's true that xeriscape plants don't like to stand in wet soil. No plant survives with zero water, however, so xeriscape really refers to plants that even in dry climates require little or no watering beyond that supplied by nature.

You can grow xeriscape plants in any region, as long as you give them well-drained soil. These plants include cacti, salvias, oenotheras, any number of herbaceous perennials, bulbs, grasses, and even some trees. Bear in mind that even the most "xeriscapish" of plants will need some added watering during especially dry years. And some cacti, such as opuntias, are coastal in origin and actually benefit from more frequent watering.

Drought-tolerant

These are plants that can survive on less than 1 in. of added water above their root mass for each week of a drought. Unlike xeriscape plants, which are accustomed to dry weather most of the time, drought-tolerant plants are adapted to fairly infrequent periods of dry weather and actually thrive in conditions where there is no drought. These plants are quite numerous. The most common are varieties of dianthus, echinacea, asters, liatris, and others plants of grassland, meadow, and Mediterranean—rather than deep-forest—origin.

The tough constitution of, from front to back, daylilies, English lavender, and Russian sage make them great candidates for a xeriscape garden.

Spectrum of Plant Drought Tolerances

XERISCAPE	DROUGHT-TOLERANT	DROUGHT-INTOLERANT
Dry-climate plants	**Plants adapted to infrequent dry weather**	**Plants adapted to damp, wet climates**
• prefer infrequent waterings • low water requirements • thrive in chronically dry soil Water needs: rare deep watering	• adaptable to fairly infrequent watering • moderate water requirements • thrive in drought-free conditions, but can survive moderate drought Water needs: occasional deep watering	• must not experience drought during growing season • heavy water requirements • thrive in wet, moist, or boggy soils Water needs: regular deep watering

Drought-intolerant

This group of plants can't withstand prolonged drought, period. Some of the more delicate hostas, many ferns, and many plants of forest, bog, or swamp origin fall into this category. Most of them require 1 in. or more of applied water above the root mass each week; they will not thrive in soil that is chronically dry.

DENSITY

Lawns, beds of annuals, vegetable patches, and farm row crops tend to be densely planted from the very beginning, and tend to benefit from frequent but not terribly deep watering. Over-head sprays are usually appropriate for these types of plants.

Most horticultural designs (including perennial flower beds, ground cover areas, hedge lines, bulb displays, and trees) and even some agricultural ones (orchards and groves) survive more than a single season, and start out being planted a fair distance apart. They tend to benefit from the deep watering provided by sprays, drippers, and soakers.

DEMAND TIMES

Most plants will lose some root mass in the process of being transplanted, and a seedling is in the process of building root mass—in both cases, more frequent initial watering will make it easier for the plants to root out and establish themselves rapidly. Over time, their root masses will become fuller and more intricately developed. When the plants have settled in, you should provide less frequent but deeper watering, to encourage root growth.

Over the years, as the root systems of individual perennials, ground covers, and trees grow, the individual plants will become increasingly drought-tolerant and your waterings can become even more infrequent. The highly developed root matrix of adult plants is a bulwark against erosion in times of too much water and against withering in times of too little water.

Blooms tend to be among the plant's more fragile structures—so fragile that water on the blossoms can, through the refraction of sunlight, have a magnifying lens effect, burning the bloom. This is even more

reason to water established plants deeper, less frequently, and further away from the heat of the day.

Even when plants are dormant, you still need to water a very dry or windy spot. You don't want the roots to dry out. As we've said, cool, dry, windy weather can be particularly deceptive—

Remedial Watering

How can you tell if you're watering too much or too little? This question is not as easy to answer as you might think.

In general, plants receiving too little water will usually look limp and wilted, or roll their leaves. If plants are being watered too heavily, their leaves will often turn yellow and fall off. (See the chart below.)

However, plants can look limp and wilted for other reasons—pest damage, for one. Some plants with rigid leaves or stems don't wilt even when they are

dying of thirst. Yellowed leaves can be caused by micronutrient deficiencies. Sometimes leaves will curl or roll up as a response to overwatering.

How can you determine the culprit? Once you have identified a plant that is failing to thrive or is clearly dying, the best diagnostic method is to dig with your fingers in the soil around the base of the plant. If the plant is looking limp and the soil is very dry, increase your watering and see if the plant's health improves. If the plant's leaves are yellowed

and the soil around its base is heavily saturated with water, try cutting back on your watering.

If the leaves are yellowed and the soil is not overly wet, the plant is most likely suffering from a micronutrient deficiency. Citrus trees in unamended western clay soils, for instance, are particularly prone to this. In these situation it is probably a good idea to top-dress the plant with micronutrients or to spray the leaves with plant food.

Basic Diagnostic Chart:
Overwatering and Underwatering

LEAF CONDITION	yellow or falling off	limp, curled, or wilted	yellow
SOIL CONDITION	wet	dry	dry
CAUSE	overwatering	underwatering	micronutrient deficiency

and destructive (see p. 30). Remember, just because the plant is dormant above ground doesn't mean that its roots aren't active below. In fact, some of the most active root growth of the yearly cycle occurs when the above-ground portion of the plant appears least active. That's why some of the best times to apply fertilizers and top dresses to the soil are precisely when the plant is "dormant."

Yard History and Future

The final factor to consider before installing or changing an irrigation system is the landscape itself. Gardens evolve over time. From lawns to orchards, established crop spaces have different watering needs than new spaces. Whenever you take out a bed or replace a shrub line, your watering regime will change.

Think of your landscape not only in terms of space but also of time. Once your landscaping is grown in, will that affect the efficiency of your irrigation system? Will trees or shrubs block your spray heads and throw shadows through your spray pattern? Will you need to change to taller or different heads 5 or 10 years down the line? Always try to take the long view—you'll save yourself toil and trouble later.

NEW GROWING AREAS
You have a chance to put your personal stamp on your

landscape when you're planning a new growing space, whether it's a bed, lawn, field, or orchard. Similarly, when you install irrigation in an area where it has never existed, you have complete control over that system. All the praise and blame are yours, so make that system out of the best and most appropriate materials you can afford. Dig your trenches deep. Put in drain plug purge valves if your area exper-iences hard freezes (see p. 24). Don't stint on glue for the PVC pipes or on Teflon tape for your threaded parts. Use the best, most appropriate parts for valve manifolds, piping, and spray heads.

For lawns, trees, shrubs, and rose gardens, once you've set up your irrigation you're finished—if you decide you'll never alter your landscape. But you should monitor your plants' growth and how it affects your irrigation throw pattern. For bulbs and perennials in particular, you will see that an evolving landscape requires a flexible irrigation system. The gentle rain of microspray is appropriate during the first three to five years, but once the landscape has matured you would do well to change to a more robust and easily maintained macro system, such as stream rotors, which will let you water less frequently but more deeply.

Keep the future in mind. Once your landscape is established and grown in, you may find you want to dig up that bulb bed because the tulips and daffodils have become too crowded. You may want to dig up that section of lawn and convert it to flower beds—who can say?

ESTABLISHED GROWING AREAS

We generally consider a bulb bed or perennial stand to be established in about three years' time, a hedge line in five years, and an orchard in seven years. These are rules of thumb and somewhat conservative. "Established" is not the same thing as fully mature, but rather an indication that particular plants have settled in and are thriving. In most of these cases, you can usually begin converting to a "less frequent and deeper" watering schedule earlier than these cutoff points. How do you know if your plants are ready? Experiment with less frequent but deeper waterings after your plants have been in the ground for at least a year, and observe how they react to the change.

Annual flower beds, vegetable patches, and row crops settle in quickly, though they are never really established, since they last only a year. After peak watering around germination or transplantation, watering can often be tapered off as the crop approaches harvest, and cut off completely after harvest.

REWORKING ESTABLISHED GROWING SPACES

Growing areas for annuals are "retrofitted" with new plants virtually every year. However, real, labor-intensive retrofitting is something that usually takes place in longer-term growing areas. Revising and reworking an established landscape is a challenging task.

Similarly, a thorough overhaul of an existing irrigation system will probably require various degrees of the trenching work, pipe-cutting, and pipe-gluing usually associated with installing a new system. You will also have the roots and low-hanging branches of the established landscape to deal with while you're working.

Most property owners with irrigation systems in their yards only know enough to think that they can't "do irrigation" themselves. Many homeowners are daunted by the idea of designing and trenching out a system. Others are overwhelmed by the sub-fields, including plumbing and electrical work, that are part of landscape irrigation.

But you don't need to be a master plumber, electrician, or construction engineer to design, build, and maintain your own irrigation system. A trench is not the Channel Tunnel, the electrical work is not much more challenging than changing a light bulb, and the plumbing only involves cutting, gluing, and threading plastic pipes and connectors. By following the instructions in Chapters 3 and 4, you can design an irrigation system for the landscape that you really want—not just the one you're willing to "settle for."

CHAPTER 3

The First Stage: Bringing Water to the Manifold

This chapter will give you step-by-step instructions for connecting to your household water source. However, we should first take a moment to discuss the manifold of your irrigation system.

Mechanical, electronic, or electromechanical control of passive water flow takes place at the valve manifold. It's the primary automation site, the "command and control" center for your system as a whole.

Eventually, through the use of tensiometers and feedback control systems, irrigation control will probably become increasingly decentralized and the individual sprinkling or dripping units more autonomous. For the foreseeable future, however, irrigation control will remain centered around the operation of the manifold.

Although constructing a manifold does require you to think spatially, it's not rocket science by any means.

Designing
the Manifold

All an irrigation manifold really does is turn a single inflow pipeline into several—usually two to six—outflow pipelines. It does this through an array of control valves and associated pipelines.

LANDSCAPE ZONES

You can easily put in more than one manifold, if you need to—say, one in your front area and one in the back. This is especially appropriate if you're going to irrigate more than six different zones, requiring more than six control valves. A zone is an area hooked into the same sprinkler line and controlled by the same valve. It often consists of only one crop—a lawn section or a perennial bed section—but it can include more than one if the plants being watered have similar needs. Remember to leave yourself one or two extra control valve stations for future projects you may not have envisioned as yet.

MANIFOLD PLACEMENT

At the outset of your irrigation project, you should think about where you want the manifolds to go. When we installed Howard's system, we put in two manifolds—an array of five control valves in the front yard and a second array of four control valves in the back yard.

You should take care in deciding where to locate the valves in your yard. Position the manifold for easy access, but at the same time avoid the eyesore of all those valves marring the view.

Feel free to indulge your aesthetic inclinations. The landscape itself can serve as camouflage. In Howard's front yard, we planted a rosemary hedge to screen the manifold from view (see the photo on the facing page).

Try not to put the manifold in the ground; keep it close at hand in case any water-control problems arise. Although many people worry about working with electrical wiring, it's neither difficult nor dangerous in this context. Automated irrigation valves generally run on 12 volts—not enough to give you a serious shock.

Once you've decided where you want your irrigation manifold to be and how many stations you want it to service (usually one per zone), you're ready to decide what sprinkler heads you will need.

Choosing
Sprinkler Heads

Although irrigation consists of pipelines and spray points, effective design is not a linear process. In irrigation, as in many other aspects of life, your

A manifold is hidden from view by this rosemary hedge.

destination governs your route. As much as possible, let the placement of the sprinkler heads determine the placement of your pipes, rather than the reverse.

CROP AREAS

Before you buy a single part or dig one shovel of dirt, establish in your mind the crop areas you need to water. Don't limit yourself to flower beds and lawn areas, however. By the time you install the irrigation clock sprinkler controller (see pp. 114-118), you'll already be wanting to leave some room for future projects—a hanging basket garden, say, or fruit trees, or shrubbery.

When establishing in your mind the areas that need to be watered, mentally divide your yard into rough squares or rectangles (see Sample Irrigation Plans beginning on p. 119). This is very important when you're trying to determine which type of sprinkler head to use in a given area.

MICRO SYSTEMS

If the area to be irrigated is less than 8 ft. wide, you'll need micro systems—soaker, drip, or microspray. If the area is wider than 8 ft., you may still use a type of micro system; it depends on the types of plants to be watered. An entire front yard of perennials could be watered with microspray. Whole yards can be effectively watered using micro systems, especially in the case of ground cover areas that will not be mown.

If you have to mow a given area, even in part, and you still prefer to use a micro system because of its higher water efficiency, we suggest a macro/micro hybrid system that features microspray heads on a pop-up body (see p. 16).

MACRO SYSTEMS

Conventional pop-up systems also can service spaces that are more than 8 ft. but less than 15 ft. across. Generally, if the rectangular area is more than 15 ft. wide, we recommend you use gear-driven multi-stream rotor heads of a pop-up design, which are aesthetically pleasing. Impact heads may also be used, but stream rotors and similar gear-driven heads are considerably more water-efficient. Impact heads work well if you're more interested in putting large quantities of water on the ground in a short period of time than in placing water specifically and efficiently (such as in the salt-busting operations mentioned on p. 29).

This 12-in. pop-up body is mounted to a swing joint, which ensures ease of adjustment and "invisible" placement.

One last consideration: Microspray heads are usually deployed on stationary risers. Stationary risers are cheaper per unit than pop-ups, but they don't drop out of sight when they're not operating, as pop-ups do. Once your plants have grown in, stationary risers are often nearly as invisible as pop-ups in your no-mow areas. However, if irrigation "invisibility" is an absolute necessity for you, you should use 12-in. pop-ups instead (see the photo on the facing page).

Envisioning how your irrigation system will look above ground will help you decide how it will look underground. But first you must determine your household water pressure, and decide how you will connect to your water source.

Determining Household Water Power

Pressures and flow rates coming into homes are by no means uniform across the United States. Nationwide, water pressures in urban areas hover around 35 psi. Flow rates usually start around 5 gpm. However, there is wide variation. To be on the safe side, we recommend that you go to the minor trouble of determining flow and pressure rates on the site where you'll be building your irrigation system.

DETERMINING FLOW RATE

The easiest way to determine flow rate is to take a 5-gal. bucket, hang it on the pipe, hose bibb, or wellhead you will be working off, and let the flow come out full force. Have a partner time how long it takes for the bucket to fill. From there it's simple math: If the bucket takes 10 seconds to fill, then your gpm is gallons/seconds times 60, or $5/10 \times 60 = 30$ gpm. You can contact your city water engineer and ask what the average gpm is for your area, if you feel the need to double-check your figures (and are on city water).

If you are working off your own wellhead and have a fairly low flow—say, 10 gpm or less—we strongly recommend that you put in a storage tank, preferably at the highest possible elevation on your property. This will improve your flow rate and can also be used to improve your water pressure.

DETERMINING PRESSURE

Determining pressure is even easier than measuring flow. Go to your hardware store, buy a $5 pressure gauge, stick it on your hose bibb or wellhead pipe, and make sure no water is running anywhere else in the house or on the property. Then just turn on the water at the site where you want to measure the pressure.

The process only becomes more complicated if your land has considerable slope. Water pressure increases 1 lb. psi for every 2.3 ft. of vertical drop, and decreases by a like amount for the same amount of vertical rise.

REGULATING PRESSURE

Some sites have low pressure; others have pressure that's too high. In either case, you have several options for regulating water pressure.

New wells

If you are in a situation where you're thinking of developing a property with considerable slope and you plan to put in a well,

choose a site closest to the highest point on your property. Put in a storage tank, as close as practically possible to the highest point. This will allow you to take advantage of "gravity feed." If your property has 70 ft. to 80 ft. of vertical drop, you will be able to run most irrigation systems without having to buy a special pressurizing tank. We'll discuss this further in the section on working off a wellhead (see pp. 62-63).

City water

If you have city water coming out at high head pressure but also have considerable slope, you may need a pressure regulator along your water lines to ensure that the spray heads farthest downhill don't get water-hammered or spray so hard that their droplets implode into fog.

When you buy a pressure regulator, you're essentially paying money to steal from yourself: When pressure drops, you lose flow. If, however, you feel confident enough with your mathematical abilities, you can use your brain to regulate pressure without impeding water flow. Instead of trying to control pressure from the input end, you can control it from the output end by putting enough microspray heads, bubblers, or drippers on the line to disperse the pressure. Simply multiply the number of heads you wish to put on a line by the flow rate per head (usually listed in gallons

A pressure gauge is inexpensive and easy to operate.

per hour for microspray heads, bubblers, and drippers), then check this against the flow and pressure chart to make sure you're in the safe range.

You'll need to take into account pressure loss if the site you're irrigating is large and flat (over an acre, say). Movement of water through pipes, fittings, and water meters causes pressure loss due to friction between the water and the interior surfaces of the system. The smaller the inside diameter of a pipe, the more pressure is lost to friction per 100 ft. of distance traveled in that pipe.

Micro and macro systems
The "low and slow" aspect of micros also raises the issue of pressure regulation. Most urban and suburban housing developments have water pressures ranging from 25 psi to 50 psi. The national average for urban and suburban areas is about 35 psi. Unfortunately, that pressure is too high for many micro irrigation technologies. That's why the manufacturers often suggest that you install a pressure regulator on your micro lines.

All of this becomes an issue for one reason: Different irrigation strategies require different pressures and flows. In general, the farther a system throws from the spray head, the more pressure is required to operate it.

Micro systems with essentially zero throw, such as bubblers, drippers, and soaker line, require the least pressure. Microspray heads with a throw of less than 8 ft. require more pressure than drippers and soaker lines, but less than multi-stream rotor heads or conventional pop-ups throwing 8 ft. to 30 ft. A minimum pressure also is required to operate a pop-up head; this varies from manufacturer to manufacturer. Water guns, impact heads, and single-stream rotors throwing 30 ft. or more require the highest pressures of all.

Crop ties in here, too. Let's say you have low water pressure and a large area to be irrigated. It would be less costly and labor-intensive for you to maintain an orchard, which could be watered with drip, than a lawn the same size, which would have to be watered with a macro system.

We have included two sample charts on pp. 48 and 49 for the pipe types we work with most often—Schedule 40 PVC and poly hose. We take up the issue of frictional pressure more fully in the section on pipe diameters and sizing on pp. 79-83. A pressure-loss chart for water meters can be found on p. 132.

Pressure Loss Due to Friction for Schedule 40 PVC

psi loss per 100 ft. of pipe

Size	½ in.		¾ in.		1 in.		1¼ in.		1½ in.		2 in.		2½ in.		3 in.		4 in.	
OD	0.840		1.050		1.315		1.660		1.900		2.375		2.875		3.500		4.500	
ID	0.622		0.824		1.049		1.380		1.610		2.067		2.469		3.068		4.026	
WALL THK.	0.109		0.113		0.133		1.140		0.145		0.154		0.203		0.216		0.237	
Flow gpm	Velocity FPS	psi loss	Velocity FPS	psi loss	Velocity FPS	psi loss	Velocity FPS	psi loss	Velocity FPS	psi loss	Velocity FPS	psi loss	Velocity FPS	psi loss	Velocity FPS	psi loss	Velocity FPS	psi loss
1	1.05	0.43	0.60	0.11	0.37	0.03	0.21	0.01	0.15	0.00								
2	2.11	1.55	1.20	0.39	0.74	0.12	0.42	0.03	0.31	0.02	0.19	0.00						
3	3.16	3.28	1.80	0.84	1.11	0.26	0.64	0.07	0.47	0.03	0.28	0.01	0.20	0.00				
4	4.22	5.60	2.40	1.42	1.48	0.44	0.85	0.12	0.62	0.05	0.38	0.02	0.26	0.01				
5	5.27	8.46	3.00	2.15	1.85	0.66	1.07	0.18	0.78	0.08	0.47	0.02	0.33	0.01	0.21	0.00		
6	6.33	11.86	3.60	3.02	2.22	0.93	1.28	0.25	0.94	0.12	0.57	0.03	0.40	0.01	0.26	0.01		
7	7.38	15.77	4.20	4.01	2.59	1.24	1.49	0.33	1.10	0.15	0.66	0.05	0.46	0.02	0.30	0.01		
8	8.44	20.20	4.80	5.14	2.96	1.59	1.71	0.42	1.25	0.20	0.76	0.06	0.53	0.02	0.34	0.01		
9	9.49	25.12	5.40	6.39	3.33	1.97	1.92	0.52	1.41	0.25	0.85	0.07	0.60	0.03	0.39	0.01		
10	10.55	30.54	6.00	7.77	3.70	2.40	2.14	0.63	1.57	0.30	0.95	0.09	0.66	0.04	0.43	0.01		
11	11.60	36.43	6.60	9.27	4.07	2.86	2.35	0.75	1.73	0.36	1.05	0.11	0.73	0.04	0.47	0.02		
12	12.65	42.80	7.21	10.89	4.44	3.36	2.57	0.89	1.88	0.42	1.14	0.12	0.80	0.05	0.52	0.02	0.30	0.00
14	14.76	56.94	8.41	14.48	5.19	4.47	2.99	1.18	2.20	0.56	1.33	0.17	0.93	0.07	0.60	0.02	0.35	0.01
16	16.87	72.92	9.61	18.55	5.93	5.73	3.42	1.51	2.51	0.71	1.52	0.21	1.07	0.09	0.69	0.03	0.40	0.01
18	18.98	90.69	10.81	23.07	6.67	7.13	3.85	1.88	2.83	0.89	1.71	0.26	1.20	0.11	0.78	0.04	0.45	0.01
20	21.09	110.23	12.01	28.04	7.41	8.66	4.28	2.28	3.14	1.08	1.90	0.32	1.33	0.13	0.86	0.05	0.50	0.01
22			13.21	33.45	8.15	10.33	4.71	2.72	3.46	1.29	2.10	0.38	1.47	0.16	0.95	0.06	0.55	0.01
24			14.42	39.30	8.89	12.14	5.14	3.20	3.77	1.51	2.29	0.45	1.60	0.19	1.04	0.07	0.60	0.02
26			15.62	45.58	9.64	14.08	5.57	3.17	4.09	1.75	2.48	0.52	1.74	0.22	1.12	0.08	0.65	0.02
28			16.82	52.28	10.38	16.15	5.99	4.25	4.40	2.01	2.67	0.60	1.87	0.25	1.21	0.09	0.70	0.02
30			18.02	59.41	11.12	18.35	6.42	4.83	4.72	2.28	2.86	0.68	2.00	0.29	1.30	0.10	0.75	0.03
35			12.97	24.42	7.49	6.43	5.50	3.04	3.34	0.90	2.34	0.38	1.51	0.13	0.88	0.04	0.38	0.00
40					14.83	31.27	8.56	8.23	6.29	3.89	3.81	1.15	2.67	0.49	1.73	0.17	1.00	0.01
45					16.68	38.89	9.64	10.24	7.08	4.84	4.29	1.43	3.01	0.60	1.95	0.21	1.13	0.06
50					18.53	47.27	10.71	12.45	7.87	5.88	4.77	1.74	3.34	0.73	2.16	0.26	1.25	0.07
55							11.78	14.85	8.65	7.01	5.25	2.08	3.68	0.88	2.38	0.30	1.38	0.08

Note: Shaded areas of chart indicate velocities over 5 ft. per second (FPS). Use with caution.

Velocity of flow values are computed from the general equation $V = 0.408 \dfrac{Q}{d^2}$

Friction pressure loss values are computed from the equation $h_f = 0.2083 \left(\dfrac{100}{C}\right)^{1.852} \dfrac{Q^{1.852}}{d^{4.866}}$ x 0.433 for psi loss per 100 ft. of pipe

Pressure Loss Due to Friction for Polyethylene Hose

psi loss per 100 ft. of tube

Size	½ in.		¾ in.		1 in.		1¼ in.		1½ in.		2 in.		2½ in.		3 in.		4 in.	
ID	0.622		0.824		1.049		1.380		1.610		2.067		2.469		3.068		4.026	
Flow gpm	Velocity FPS	psi loss	Velocity FPS	psi loss	Velocity FPS	psi loss	Velocity FPS	psi loss	Velocity FPS	psi loss	Velocity FPS	psi loss	Velocity FPS	psi loss	Velocity FPS	psi loss	Velocity FPS	psi loss
1	1.05	0.49	0.60	0.12	0.37	0.04	0.21	0.01	0.15	0.00	0.09	0.00						
2	2.10	1.76	1.20	0.45	0.74	0.14	0.42	0.04	0.31	0.02	0.19	0.01						
3	3.16	3.73	1.80	0.95	1.11	0.29	0.64	0.08	0.47	0.04	0.28	0.01	0.20	0.00				
4	4.21	6.35	2.40	1.62	1.48	0.50	0.85	0.13	0.62	0.06	0.38	0.02	0.26	0.01				
5	5.27	9.60	3.00	2.44	1.85	0.76	1.07	0.20	0.78	0.09	0.47	0.03	0.33	0.01	0.21	0.00		
6	6.32	13.46	3.60	3.43	2.22	1.06	1.28	0.28	0.94	0.13	0.57	0.04	0.40	0.02	0.26	0.01		
7	7.38	17.91	4.20	4.56	2.59	1.41	1.49	0.37	1.10	0.18	0.66	0.05	0.46	0.02	0.30	0.01		
8	8.43	22.93	4.80	5.84	2.96	1.80	1.71	0.47	1.25	0.22	0.76	0.07	0.53	0.03	0.34	0.01		
9	9.49	28.52	5.40	7.26	3.33	2.24	1.92	0.59	1.41	0.28	0.85	0.08	0.60	0.03	0.39	0.01		
10	10.54	34.67	6.00	8.82	3.70	2.73	2.14	0.72	1.57	0.34	0.95	0.10	0.66	0.04	0.43	0.01		
11	11.60	41.36	6.60	10.53	4.07	3.25	2.35	0.86	1.73	0.40	1.05	0.12	0.73	0.05	0.47	0.02	0.27	0.00
12	12.66	48.60	7.21	12.37	4.44	3.82	2.57	1.01	1.88	0.48	1.14	0.14	0.80	0.06	0.52	0.02	0.30	0.01
14	14.76	64.65	8.41	16.46	5.19	5.08	2.99	1.34	2.20	0.63	1.33	0.19	0.93	0.08	0.60	0.03	0.35	0.01
16	16.87	82.79	9.61	21.07	5.93	6.51	3.42	1.71	2.51	0.81	1.52	0.24	1.07	0.10	0.69	0.04	0.40	0.01
18	18.98	02.97	10.81	26.21	6.67	8.10	3.85	2.13	2.83	1.01	1.71	0.30	1.20	0.13	0.78	0.04	0.45	0.01
20			12.01	31.86	7.41	9.84	4.28	2.59	3.14	1.22	1.90	0.36	1.33	0.15	0.86	0.05	0.50	0.01
22			13.21	38.01	8.15	11.74	4.71	3.09	3.46	1.46	2.10	0.43	1.47	0.18	0.95	0.06	0.55	0.02
24			14.42	44.65	8.89	13.79	5.14	3.63	3.77	1.72	2.29	0.51	1.60	0.21	1.04	0.07	0.60	0.02
26			15.62	41.79	9.64	16.00	5.57	4.21	4.09	1.99	2.48	0.59	1.74	0.25	1.12	0.09	0.65	0.02
28			16.82	59.41	10.38	18.35	5.99	4.83	4.40	2.28	2.67	0.68	1.87	0.29	1.21	0.10	0.70	0.03
30			18.02	67.50	11.12	20.85	6.42	5.49	4.72	2.59	2.86	0.77	2.00	0.32	1.30	0.11	0.75	0.03
35					12.97	27.74	7.49	7.31	5.50	3.45	3.34	1.02	2.34	0.43	1.51	0.15	0.88	0.04
40					14.83	35.53	8.56	9.36	6.29	4.42	3.81	1.31	2.67	0.55	1.73	0.19	1.00	0.05
45					16.68	44.19	9.64	11.64	7.08	5.50	4.29	1.63	3.01	0.69	1.95	0.24	1.13	0.06
50					18.53	53.71	10.71	14.14	7.87	6.68	4.77	1.98	3.34	0.83	2.16	0.29	1.25	0.08
55							11.78	16.87	8.65	7.97	5.25	2.36	3.68	1.00	2.38	0.35	1.38	0.09

Note: Shaded areas of chart indicate velocities over 5 ft. per second (FPS). Use with caution.

Velocity of flow values are computed from the general equation $V = 0.408 \dfrac{Q}{d^2}$

Friction pressure loss values are computed from the equation $h_f = 0.2083 \left(\dfrac{100}{C}\right)^{1.852} \dfrac{Q^{1.852}}{d^{4.866}}$ x 0.433 for psi loss per 100 ft. of pipe

Tapping in for Your Irrigation Line

Now that you have envisioned the irrigation design for your property and have determined how much water pressure is at your disposal, you're ready to make a very important, even potentially critical, decision: Should you tap into the main water line before it enters your house or should you work off a hose bibb?

This requires a bit of fore-thought. As Peter Hemp notes in his book *Plumbing a House*, "Rough plumbing isn't very often installed by non-plumbers, other than an occasional general contractor." However, with irrigation, the situation is exactly the opposite—most irrigation systems in the United States are installed by non-plumbers. In fact, most irrigation systems, particularly in the Southwest, are installed by landscapers employing low-skilled manual laborers.

The first thing you need to do is familiarize yourself with the plumbing code for your area. Once you understand local regulations on cutting into main household water lines, you can make the critical decision of where to begin your irrigation system. Irrigation systems are generally less regulated and restricted by codes than plumbing systems are; they don't directly involve water flow within human habitations. Plumbing code information is available at your local library. Call your city or county building inspector to see if your locale has any restrictions regarding tapping into household water lines for landscape irrigation. Most do not have restrictions. In the few locales that do, the solution is simply to work off an existing hose bibb. Restrictions are even more minimal if you are putting in a well or working off an established wellhead.

THE MAIN HOUSEHOLD LINE

Tapping directly into the main water line lets you keep household water systems and yard irrigation systems as separate as possible. Another advantage is that main water lines run pipe that is at least ¾ in. in diameter, while bibbs generally run smaller pipe—often only ½ in. That step-down in size means a decrease in available water flow coming through your irrigation pipes. The bends and twists of the water line as it travels through the house also tend to reduce flow at the bibb. The biggest disadvantages to working with the main line are that you have to find the pipe-line, dig it up, and cut into it.

Locating the main line

Let's say you've decided to tap directly into the main line coming from the street to the house. You first have to establish the location of the pipe. Usually you'll find it next to the water meter, but if you live in an area without meters, you'll have to search around the property a little bit. The best places to look are near the curb by the street, and where the pipe enters the house. Check the basement, if you have one. If your house is built on a slab, check the point where the pipe rises to enter the house—usually the wall closest to the nearest street.

Digging into the main line

When you've found the main line, you will need to expose an area around the pipe that's approximately 2 ft. to 3 ft. long and 1 ft. to 2 ft. across. This will give you enough room to work with the pipe easily. Get your shovel (preferably a trenching shovel or another strong, narrow-bladed shovel) and start digging.

Once you've cleared a work space around the pipe, you should be able to estimate the diameter of the pipe and to establish whether the pipe is copper, galvanized, or PVC. Galvanized and PVC are easier to work with than copper (unless you feel comfortable with a blowtorch and molten lead). If your main line is copper, we suggest you get a trained plumber to insert and affix a straight tee to a ¾-in. gate valve, with female or male pipe thread to screw into or onto.

Don't reduce the pipe size if you find that you have pipe larger than ¾ in. You can do that later, when you reach the manifold.

Next, write up a parts list and go to your local irrigation or plumbing supply store. You may feel a little intimidated the first time you walk into one of those big, hangar-like hardware stores, or even into a small irrigation supply shop. You'll see shelf after shelf of pipes, couplers, and spray heads. Bear in mind that there are only a few basic irrigation systems, and they can all be adapted to suit your personal needs—as in the aforementioned hybrid micro/macro system (see p. 16). And don't be afraid to ask the experts at the store for help. (It also may help to review pp. 52-53 before you go shopping.)

Once you have your parts, you're ready to tap into your main line.

Tapping into a Main Line: A Parts List

By tapping into your main household water line, you can maximize water flow for your irrigation system. Here are the parts you will need to tap into a main water line:

• A compression tee (also called a G fitting or slip union tee), ¾ in. or 1 in. in diameter (see the photos below). This part works well for galvanized or PVC. Make sure that each end of the tee has a screw-on capping piece outside and a rubber gasket inside. Without this gasket or "O-ring," the compression ring will spew water and will never clamp down fully on the pipe. Make sure an O-ring is present for both ends.

• A ball valve or gate valve, ¾ in. or 1 in. in diameter. Although each valve has a similar function, they're actually different parts. Since a ball valve swivels a holed ball or "globe" open or shut, it has fewer moving parts; the position of the valve handle tells you whether the valve is open or shut (see the top photos on the facing page). A gate valve incrementally adjusts water flow in response to a blocking gate that moves into or out of blocking position when you crank a handle. Because that handle is usually circular, it's harder to tell if a gate valve is open or shut just by looking at it (see the facing page).

Gate valves are fine for when you want incremental control of water flow (to a garden hose, for instance), but ball valves are more appropriate in this context because we are creating an on/off switch for the irrigation system. Ball valves also are less prone than gate valves to getting grit in the mechanism and leaking. However, ball valves are considerably more expensive.

Whether you choose a gate valve or a ball valve, the valve size must match the size of your main line pipe.

• A small pipe section known as a nipple (see the bottom photos on the facing page). Buy one longer than 1 in. so you can work a pipe wrench on it.

• A hacksaw.

• Two pipe wrenches.

• Teflon tape.

• A sturdy pair of PVC pipe cutters. You could cut your PVC pipe with the hacksaw, but that leaves particulate matter in the line that could cause clogging. PVC pipe cutters make a clean cut, and they're easier to use in cramped areas.

Remember, always buy extra parts. Most of the time you'll be working with PVC, which is cheap; buy one or two more of everything than you think you'll need.

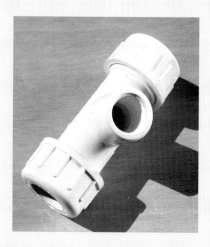

Close-up of a compression tee.

A ¾-in. compression tee, disassembled to show screw-on endpieces and rubber O-ring gaskets.

A ball valve in the "on" position.

A ball valve in the "off" position.

A gate valve, shown here flushing a main line junction.

These male pipe threads of a nipple piece are being wrapped with Teflon tape to lubricate the threads and prevent leaks. Make sure you wrap the tape in the direction of the insertion.

Here, Teflon-taping for one set or "side" of male pipe threads on a nipple has just been completed.

Using a Hacksaw

1. Prep the area to be sawed with oil—it reduces friction.

2. Cut through the pipe with a hacksaw (galvanized pipe is shown here). This is a tabletop mock-up. It's a challenge in the trenches!

3. Oil the pipe again as you continue to cut.

5. A finished cut through galvanized pipe.

4. Continue with a few more hacksaw strokes.

Steps for tapping into the main line

1. First, be sure to switch off your household water supply at the street. Whenever you're going to be cutting "live" lines, turn them off—you don't want water spraying all over the place.

2. Take your hacksaw, select a location on the exposed main pipe line, and, using the hacksaw, mark the area to be cut. Dab the marked area with oil. This will reduce friction, particularly from metal filings, and make cutting easier. Make two cuts, 1½ in. to 2 in. apart, creating a gap in the main water pipe.

3. Unscrew your compression tee into its component parts: endpieces, gaskets, and body, as shown in the photo on p. 52.

4. Slide each compression tee endpiece onto the pipe on either side of the gap you've created. The endpieces should have their screw threads facing in, toward the gap in the pipe (see the top photo at right).

5. Put the gaskets on, sliding and pushing each gasket a couple of inches up the pipe on either side of the gap (see the center photo at right).

6. Place the body of the compression tee so that the pipe on either side of the gap is going into the tee (see the bottom photo at right). If you find you haven't left yourself a large

The endpieces of the compression tee have been pushed down either end of the gap in the main water pipe line.

The endpieces and rubber O-ring gaskets have been placed on the pipe in preparation for the compression tee body.

The endpieces, gaskets, and body of the compression tee are ready to be screwed together.

The compression tee is in place on the pipe.

Screw the wrapped nipple into the compression tee.

enough gap, take the body off and cut a bit more of the main water pipe. Be careful not to cut too much off your main water pipe; you could create a gap that's too large to be covered by your compression tee.

7. Position the body of the tee so the socket is parallel to the ground, facing neither up nor down.

8. Screw each endpiece to the body of the compression tee (see the top photo at left). This may take several tries, since you'll have to adjust the positions of the compression tee, the water pipe, and the endpiece. As you screw the endpieces to the body, the gaskets should clamp down on their respective sections of pipe, sealing the compression tee to the main line. What was a gap is now ready to become a new branch line—your main irrigation line.

9. Take the nipple, which should have male pipe threads on both ends, and wrap those threads with Teflon tape. (Male pipe thread screws *into*, while female pipe thread screws *over*.) The tape helps guard against leaks. Be sure to wrap the tape in the direction of insertion for the pipe threads, not against it.

10. Thread (turn) one end of the wrapped nipple into the socket of the compression tee (see the bottom photo at left). Screw the nipple just a little beyond hand-

tight. Give it a turn with the pipe wrench, but be careful not to exert too much force.

11. Thread the valve, either gate or ball, onto the remaining end of the nipple (see the photos at right). Hand-tighten the valve, then give it one or two more turns with a pipe wrench. The entire assembly may rotate, but this is merely taking up slack. Tighten enough to ensure against leakage, but take care not to break the plastic fittings.

12. Now you can turn the water supply for your house back on. The valve allows you to keep your domestic water "on line" while you're installing or working on your irrigation. The master control point for your irrigation system is now in place, but you're not quite done yet.

13. Look carefully for any water leaking out of the compression tee, particularly where the endpieces are tightened to the main pipe and where the endpieces are screwed onto the body of the tee. Also examine for leaks at the junctions between the nipple and the socket of the tee, and between the nipple and the valve.

If the compression tee is leaking near the endpieces or on the pipe, shut off the water again and repeat steps 4 through 8. The endpieces just need a little more tightening; sometimes the pieces of the tee aren't quite in line with each other.

Here, a gate valve is being screwed onto a nipple.

Here, a plastic ball valve is being screwed onto a nipple.

If you see water leaking from the nipple assembly, all you probably need to do is give the assembly another turn or two with the pipe wrench. If this still doesn't do the trick, take the assembly apart, rewrap the nipple with Teflon tape, and repeat steps 9 through 12.

You have now completed the first big project of your irrigation system.

This handmade valve box will provide easy access.

Leave the area where you've been working unburied until you finish the next job, which involves routing your system to the manifold.

Ultimately you'll want to buy a valve box or build one to fit your individual needs (see the photo below). The valve box serves as an access cover for your master switch. You'll need access to the on/off valve later; you'll be turning the system on and off repeatedly when you're working with the manifold. Also, you will need access in the future if you ever decide to add a component to your irrigation system. The valve box protects the valve from the weather and from accidental burial during irrigation or landscape work.

We'll now cover the hose bibb variant of this main irrigation control valve installation. If you've tapped the main water line, you might want to skip to p. 63.

THE HOSE BIBB
There are advantages to working off the hose bibb to establish your master irrigation control valve. You don't have to locate the main pipe, and you're probably already in a good location for putting in your manifold. The main disadvantages are the issues of reduced pipe size and reduced water flow discussed on p. 50.

Finding the bibb

First, find the hose bibb you want to work with and establish whether it is attached to copper or galvanized pipe. If the bibb is attached to copper pipe and you don't feel comfortable working with it, contact a professional plumber to install a ¾-in. gate valve with pipe thread. After that, it's simple PVC work you can handle yourself.

If you have galvanized pipe, it's easy to change the bibb into the departure point for a manifold. (When you are working with galvanized, always make sure you link to brass before you link to copper. Mounting galvanized directly to copper will result in electolysis, which can cause your pipes to break down rapidly.)

Establish the size of the pipe protruding from your wall. If you're in doubt, use a piece of string or wire to take a measurement, then bring the string or wire to the pipe supply store and use it for size comparison.

Steps for working off the hose bibb

1. Find your main water valve at the street and turn it off.

2. Using two pipe wrenches in position for counter-rotation (see the photo at right), unthread the bibb from the pipe sticking out of your wall. At this point you can easily establish whether you're looking at male or female pipe thread.

Working Off the Hose Bibb: A Parts List

To work off the hose bibb you'll need:
- Two nipples, ¾ in. in diameter and at least 2 in. long.
- A ¾-in. ball valve or gate valve (see p. 52).
- Teflon tape.
- A ¾-in. female-threaded coupler. If you have only ½-in. pipe, buy a single ½-in.-diameter nipple about 2 in. long, and either a ½-in. to ¾-in. threaded bushing or a ½-in. to ¾-in. bell reducer. If you choose a bell reducer, you'll also need a nipple ¾ in. in diameter and more than 1 in. long.

Counter-rotate your wrenches to remove the hose bibb. This prevents your internal plumbing from turning or twisting.

Here we're Teflon-taping the male threads of a ¾-in. galvanized pipe that was exposed when the bibcock was removed.

There's not much room to work in as we screw a ¾-in. gate valve directly onto a pipe stub coming out of a wall.

3. If the pipe is male-threaded, wrap the threaded portion with Teflon tape, remembering to wrap with the threads, not against them (see the photo at left above). If the pipe is female-threaded, go on to step 7. This is a good time to wrap all the male-threaded parts of the nipples with Teflon tape. Try not to set down the Teflon-taped parts any place they will get dirty. Place them in a box or paper bag, or on a rock, until you are ready to use them.

4. If the pipe coming out of the wall is ½-in. male, you'll need a coupler to make the transition from ½-in. to ¾-in. pipe. First screw in a ½-in. nipple, then

attach the ½-in. to ¾-in. bushing or bell reducer. If the pipe coming out of the wall is ¾-in. male, wrap the end of the pipe with Teflon tape and install the ¾-in. female-threaded coupler.

5. You should now be looking at a ¾-in. female fitting. Thread a ¾-in. nipple into the fitting, then thread your ¾-in. ball valve or gate valve onto the free end of the ¾-in. nipple. You can work directly off the galvanized male end coming out of the wall (see the photo at right above), but that doesn't leave you much room to work with. It's important that you have enough room between your house and the valve to turn the valve on

60

and off easily; we recommend you install a nipple. Hand-tighten everything.

6. Place the first of your two pipe wrenches on the original piece of pipe coming out of the wall. Because this pipe into the house should not turn, place your first wrench here to counter-rotate the direction that the second pipe wrench, used to screw on the assembly, will turn. Tighten the entire assembly with the second pipe wrench placed on the valve. Tighten this as firmly as you can, but try to leave the handle on the valve pointing up.

7. Turn on the main valve near the street and check for leaks. If you see any, tighten more with the pipe wrenches. If that doesn't solve the problem, switch off your water, take apart the offending pipes, wrap them with Teflon tape, and test them again. Do this until you find no more leaks.

You have now established a master irrigation control valve off a hose bibb. You will be able to switch it on and off so that you can work on your irrigation system without shutting off water to your house. You may wish to place your manifold here, since you're familiar with the area and it's free of obstructions. When building your manifold, you might want to leave space to put in a new hose bibb (see the photo at right). Otherwise, by turning your hose bibb into a manifold, you'll lose one bibb.

A four-station manifold, with a pipe elbow provided for the hose bibb.

THE WELLHEAD

The advantage to working off a wellhead is that a private well can offer the best of all possible worlds for irrigation. You essentially function as your own water company when you own your land and well. You can control pipe sizes, flow rates, and storage capacities.

Drilling

If you are considering developing raw land, you will have to think about where to put the well. Hitting water is by no means a sure thing, especially in the West. Both scientific hydrologists and preternatural "water witchers" can be wrong. Putting in a well can be an expensive gamble.

Even if you do hit water, you'll have to have it tested. There is always the possibility that the water will be neither potable nor usable for irrigation, for reasons ranging from high bacterial content to uranium or other radioactive particles in the water. At the very least, you will have to cope with the fact that well water tends to be "harder"—higher in dissolved mineral content—than water from other sources. This is a real consideration if you're contemplating using clog-prone delivery systems, such as some varieties of microspray and drip. Low-flow wells, too, will sometimes stop producing completely, long before your need of them has ended.

Storage tanks

Let's assume you already have a successful hole in the ground with water in it. You'll next have to purchase a pump, unless you're lucky enough to have an artesian well pumping for you. We recommend putting a storage tank on your property if you have a well and pump, even if your system has appreciable flow. The tank should be located at the highest available point on your property so you can use gravity feed for pressure (see p. 46).

If you are still choosing your well site, we recommend that you place your well at the highest elevation. This will eliminate the need to install more than one pump: one to pump the water out of the ground and another to pump it uphill to your storage tank.

What if you have a small property with a simple irrigation system? You can probably get away without a storage tank if you already have adequate pressure and flow. However, many properties with wells tend to be larger and more rural, and demand more complex irrigation systems. In these cases, a storage tank is a virtual necessity.

Pressurizing tanks

What if your property is flat and you can't make use of gravity feed to increase pressure? You have two options. One is a pressurizing tank, which mechanically increases the pressure of the water it holds. The disadvantages of pressurizing tanks are their cost, which can range from a few hundred to several thousand dollars; their limited capacity; and the fact that because they are mechanical, they can break down. Your other option is a water tower.

Water towers

Largely passive systems, water towers make use of the fact that water pressure increases by 1 lb. for every 2.3 ft. of vertical rise. They are less prone to mechanical breakdown than pressurizing tanks. Storage capacities in water towers can range significantly, from 100 gal. to thousands of gallons. Generally, the greater the storage capacity, the more the tower will cost. The same holds true for height: The higher your tower, the higher your construction expenses will be.

THE WELL MAIN LINE

If you already have storage, water pressure, and a residence on the property, you can tap into the main line from your water source to your residence in the manner described on pp. 50-58. If you have a well, pump, and storage tank in place, but no residence, you should use this opportunity

to go with the largest pipe size you can afford. The advantage of large pipe size—decreased loss in pressure and flow resulting from friction—will help offset some of the costs of being your own water company. For larger properties (five or more acres) we recommend that you use PVC pipe at least 2 in. in diameter— it's a good compromise between initial cost and long-term flow and pressure savings.

When you are working off an initial stub pipe (small outflow pipe) from a storage or pressurizing tank, the procedure is essentially the same as that for working off a hose bibb once the bibb has been removed, though scaled up for larger pipe sizes.

Laying Pipe from the Valve to the Manifold

Whether you're working with city water or a well, now's the time to dig trenches for your pipe. Begin by digging a trench from your master irrigation control valve to the location where the manifold will be, if it's not going to be at your wellhead or hose bibb.

Try to lay out trenches based on straight lines and 90° turns. You'll have to use a little extra pipe, but it will be easier to find your pipes later, if you ever need to dig them up or troubleshoot them. Also, most fittings are manufactured on 90° and 180° assumptions. If you're planning on more than one manifold, dig your trenches large enough to accommodate a tee (three-way) or cross (four-way) fitting—at least 5 in. wide.

Measure your distances from point to point, then go to the pipe supply store. Whenever you buy PVC pipe to be put in the ground, buy Schedule 40 (see p. 48). Buy 10 ft. to 20 ft. more pipe than you think you'll need, just to be on the safe side. Be sure to dig extra-deep trenches if you live in an area where hard freezes occur; 18 in. will suffice in most of the continental United States. In mountainous areas or in areas of extreme cold, consult the U.S. Geologic Survey, agricultural agents, and similar sources to learn average ground freezing depths in your area—then dig your pipes 6 in. deeper than that. Install purge valves in tees every

An assortment of linkages for ¾-in. and ½-in. pipe. Top row, left to right: a straight ¾-in. slip coupler, a slip-slip-slip tee, a slip-slip-thread tee, a four-way slip cross. Middle row: a ¾-in.-slip to ½-in.-slip reducing tee, a ¾-in.-slip to ½-in. threaded elbow (or ell), a ¾-in.-slip to ¾-in.-slip elbow. Bottom row, left to right: a ¾-in. slip bushing, a ¾-in. threaded plug, a ½-in. threaded nipple.

50 ft. to 100 ft. in order to prevent pipe rupture (see p. 24). Position them facing downward, as they work with gravity, not against it.

If you live in a warm climate, 1-ft. trenches are deep enough, but don't dig any shallower than that. Nothing is more discouraging than seeing your irrigation lines surfacing after a few years. Remember too that the deeper you put your pipes, the less likely you'll be to hit them with a shovel when working in your landscape.

Wherever you live, remember to buy two more of each type of fitting than you intend to use, as well as extra PVC cement (pipe glue), Teflon tape, and any other plastic supplies.

Now it's time to lay the pipe from your master irrigation control valve to the manifold.

STEPS FOR PIPE INSTALLATION

1. Dig your trench or trenches from the master valve to the point where you want to install your manifold (see the photo at right). Lay out lengths of ¾-in. Schedule 40 pipe on the ground beside the trench or trenches. When laying out the pipe, allow for about 1 ft. of overlap per 20 ft. length of pipe.

Take your climate into account when you dig a trench from the master valve to the manifold.

Laying Out 20-ft. Lengths of Pipe with 1-ft. Overlap

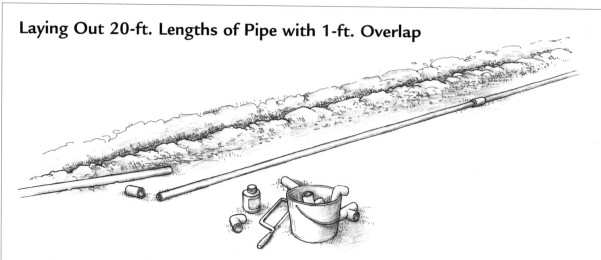

If you figure a 1-ft. overlap for each 20-ft. length of pipe, you'll have enough extra pipe for any sagging that may occur in the trench.

Threading a ¾-in. male-to-slip adapter into a ¾-in. ball valve.

You can buy cement that is specifically made for gluing PVC pipe. We're gluing (left) and inserting (above) PVC pipe into the size-matched slip side of the male adapter.

2. Place any fittings on the ground at each point where pipes and parts will need to be connected. Carry a small box or a pail that contains extra parts and any duplicates of those you've just set out.

3. Wrap one of your ¾-in. male-to-slip adapters with Teflon tape, remembering to wrap in the direction of the threads. Then thread the male end into the master ball valve or gate valve that you installed earlier in the main line (see the photo on the facing page). Use a pipe wrench to turn the male adapter a half-turn beyond hand-tight.

4. Apply glue to the inside of the female slip side of the fitting. Also apply glue liberally to the outside of the first in. or so of the pipe you wish to insert into the slip fitting (see the photos above).

Be sure not to let the glued pipe sections come into contact with the soil. You don't want to get any particulates in the pipe junctures, as that could cause leaks later. Lay a small piece of pipe across the trench to keep the glued surfaces propped safely above the soil.

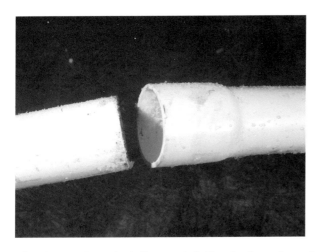

The pipe on the right is flare-ended. You don't need couplers to join lengths of flare-ended pipe—only glue.

5. Insert the male pipe end into the female slip section. Give the male part a quarter-turn when the pipe is in place, before the glue hardens. The quarter-turn smears the glue and eliminates air bubbles, which could turn into hairline leaks later.

6. Move down the trench and repeat steps 4 and 5 using ¾-in. slip-to-slip couplers. Couplers aren't necessary for pipes with flared ends—just spread glue on the inside of the flare and the outside of the pipe, as in the photos above. Glue both the insides of the couplers and the outsides of the pipes, and insert them together, repeating the process until you're at the site of your planned valve manifold. If you plan on more than one manifold, keep repeating steps 4 and 5 until you've glued all your major lengths of pipe.

7. At the manifold-site end of your pipes, glue in a ¾-in. slip L fitting, pointing up (see the left photo on the facing page). Glue the outside in. of a piece of ¾-in. Schedule 40 pipe about 3 ft. long, and insert this piece into the L, which you've glued on the inside (see the top right photo on the facing page). You now have a piece of ¾-in. PVC pipe standing vertical to the ground. Glue a slip tee to the top of the vertical piece, through the tee's socket, not through either of its ends (see the bottom right photo on the facing page). This is the pipe fixture from which you will build your valve manifold.

8. Flush out the line. Go to your master irrigation control valve and turn on the water full blast. When you see clear water flowing out of the manifold-site end of the pipe, with no globs of glue or clumps of mud, turn off

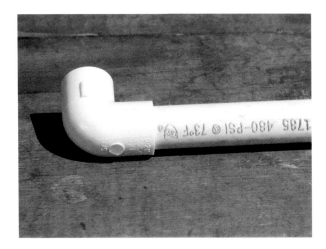

The manifold will be built on this elbow at the end of this pipe run.

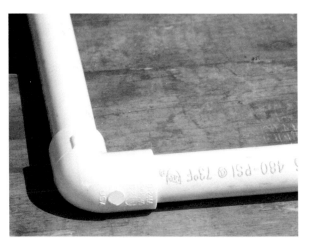

This pipe length will provide the vertical rise to the manifold.

the master irrigation valve. You will need to perform this flushing procedure when you've finished each major step of your irrigation project. These flushings are important because they prevent clogging problems.

You've just completed another important part of the project—but don't bury the pipes yet. There may still be some leaks that will be easier to find if the pipes are exposed, and you may be able to use some of the same trenches for other distribution-line work on your project.

The next step is the most challenging of all: building the valve manifold, the nexus which will give you varied and precise control over your yard and garden watering. It's at the manifold that your irrigation becomes a full-fledged system.

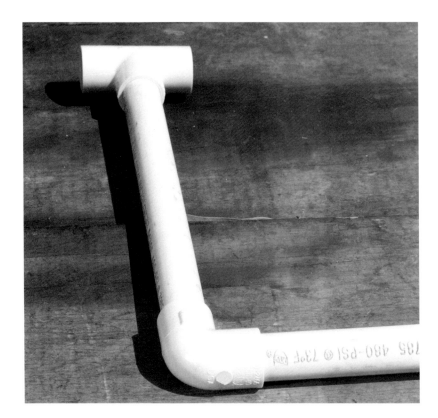

The manifold will branch from the tee at the top of the vertical pipe.

Building the Manifold

Manifolds control the horizontal distribution of water by first controlling water flow vertically. When working off PVC coming from a main line, you should think "In-Up-Valve-Down-Out": Water flows in through an ascending pipe, up into the manifold, where it encounters irrigation control valves that either stop it or allow it to move into the descending pipe on the other end of each valve. Each descending pipe attaches through an elbow to a pipeline that distributes the water horizontally to spray heads or to further distribution lines (see the drawing below).

Water Flow from a Supply Line through a Manifold

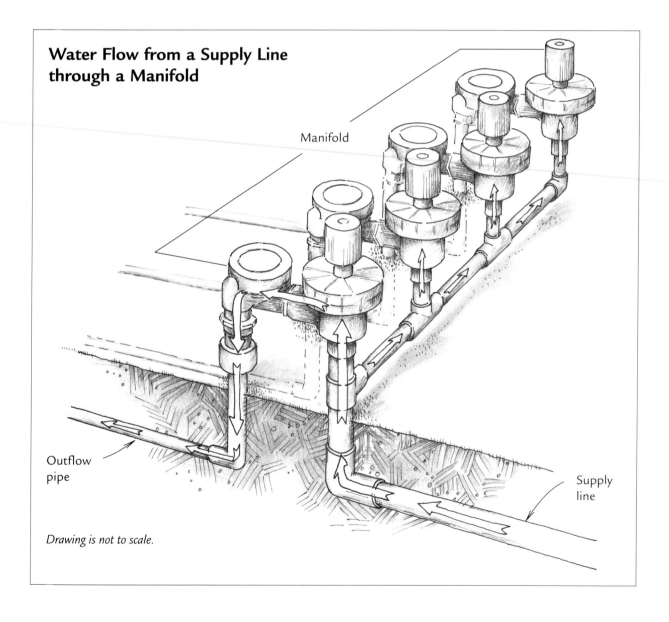

Manifold

Outflow pipe

Supply line

Drawing is not to scale.

THE MANIFOLD STRUCTURE

The manifold itself is straight-forward if you think of it in simple "Tinkertoy" terms. The most basic arrangement can be thought of this way: Ls on the ends and Ts in the middle, connected by nipples (see the top photo below). Once you add the inflow pipe the manifold is built onto, you have the basic skeleton.

The skeleton for a four-station manifold, with two stations "capped off" and available for future use.

Another view of the same skeleton. Notice the position of the downward-facing tee.

In the simplest straight-line configuration, a four-station manifold would be L(up)-T(up)-T(down)-T(up)-L(up). Each hyphen represents the short length of connecting pipe referred to as a nipple; the single downward-facing T is the one connected (in the PVC version described on p. 21) to the ascending pipe that brings the water to the manifold (see the bottom photo on p. 71 and the photos below). The L-T-L pattern can be changed to support more or fewer water lines simply by adding or subtracting Ts and connecting nipples. The pattern can also be modified into arrays other than straight lines (see the top photo on the facing page).

A note: You should lay out your manifold design as a whole before you start gluing or threading things together.

A four-station manifold skeleton with elbows, nipples, and tees, laid out in galvanized.

The same galvanized skeleton, assembled.

MATERIALS

The manifold can be made of either galvanized pipe or PVC pipe. If you are working off a hose bibb, make the manifold out of galvanized pipe so it will be a bit stronger and more rigid, and more tolerant to cold temperatures. If you live in a hard-freeze climate, the manifold should be wrapped with insulating material when it's completed, whether you're using PVC or galvanized pipe. The basic L-T-L pattern remains the same in galvanized, but the Ls, Ts, and nipples all will be threaded. This will mean a few more leaks to tighten up during the initial installation.

If you're working with PVC pipe, on the other hand, you can use either threaded PVC fittings and threaded nipples (see photo below), or slip fittings and slip-

One of many possible forms of the basic manifold skeleton.

Here, threaded nipples in black Schedule 80 PVC connect to two stations.

to-female or slip-to-male fittings (see the photo below). The advantage with slip fittings is the ease and speed with which the job can be accomplished: Nipples can be readily cut to size from Schedule 40 pipe, then quickly and easily glued into the slip fittings. The drawback becomes apparent only if you have to replace a valve or valves at a later date. You can't just unscrew things; you'll have to cut and rebuild.

Working with threaded PVC fittings and Schedule 80 nipples is just like working with always-threaded galvanized pipe. You have the easier replacement option, but you'll be more confined by the lengths and types of available fittings and nipples.

STEMS

Whether you're working with galvanized, slip PVC, or threaded PVC, you will now need a stem to connect every manifold orifice

This variant uses slip pipe nipples with a threaded male adapter atop the nipple, for threading into the female orifice at the base of the valve. Here, the two adapters on the left are capped with female-threaded end caps.

to the orifice in the bottom of each of your irrigation control valves. If you have four stations, you'll need four stems (see the photo below). A stem is a 4-in. or 5-in. length of pipe that connects the outflow of a manifold fitting to the inflow of a valve. The inflow of the valve is female-threaded. In galvanized or threaded PVC, a male-threaded nipple of appropriate diameter and length can be used to connect the female manifold fitting to the female valve orifice.

If you're working in slip PVC, cut a 4-in. or 5-in. length of PVC for each station and top it with a slip-to-male-pipe adapter (see the photo on p. 76).

When finished, you will in every case be looking at stems with male-threaded ends, as many of them as you have control valve "stations." You should make sure that you've glued, or taped and threaded, everything tightly. Do not attach the irrigation control valves yet. Instead, wrap the

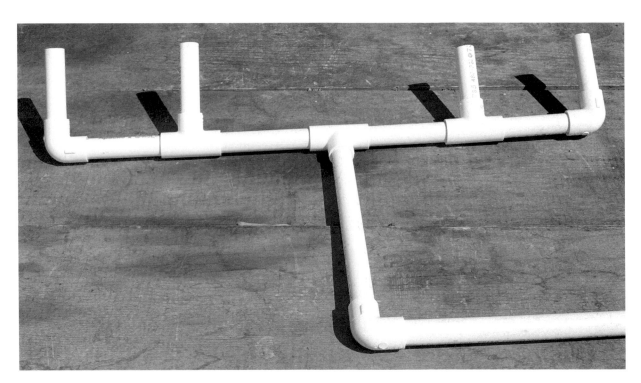

Elbows and tees, with matching stems.

male-threaded parts with Teflon tape and screw female-threaded end caps onto the male parts—but only to hand-tightness.

Turn on the water and check for leaks in the manifold. If you have a leak at a glued joint, you'll have to cut out the offending piece and redo that section. If you have a leak at a threaded joint, try using a pipe wrench to tighten it up. If that doesn't work, unthread the leaking piece, rewrap it with Teflon tape, then thread it back into or onto the manifold.

IRRIGATION CONTROL VALVES

Once you've stopped any leaks, turn off the water and remove the caps. Rewrap the male ends with fresh Teflon tape. Now you can install your irrigation control valves. These are anti-siphon valves and they can be simply threaded onto the male fittings, just as you earlier screwed the caps onto those same fittings. The only challenging part is trying to decide which orifice of the valve screws onto the male fittings. Most manufacturers mark the valves with arrows or words indicating which valve orifice attaches to the inflow side and which to the outflow. Find these indicators and let them guide you.

Stems topped with slip-female to threaded-male adapters.

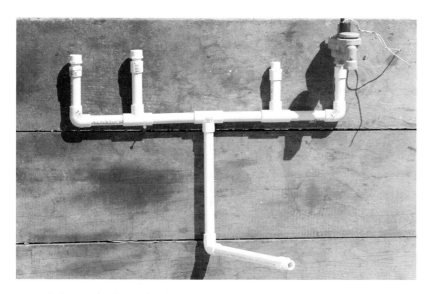

From left to right, lines that have been capped, left open, and valved.

If you aren't activating all of your valves yet, cap the male-threaded ends of the lines you're not using.

Turn on the water once again. Don't despair if water comes flooding out of the valves and flows for a minute or two. This is normal. If the water doesn't stop flowing, odds are you will simply need to tighten the bleeder valve on top of the unit. Be patient. The bleeder valve will not shut off the water instantaneously. Because people expect instant shut-off, they are prone to overtighten the bleeder valve in an attempt to make the whole valve shut off. Some are so zealous that they end up twisting off the bleeder valve's control head. Relax—at proper finger-tightness, the valve will shut off in its own good time.

If you're planning to use an automated time clock to open and shut your irrigation control valves, this is a good time to install it—you've already got an open trench that you can run wire along. If you're using a manual control system, you are now ready to move on to installing the "down-out" portion of your irrigation system.

CHAPTER 4

Tinkertoy Work: Piping Water to the Plants

In irrigation systems, water branches from a main line to the outer reaches of your landscape. When you visualize your system, it may help to think of a tree: The main irrigation line is the trunk, the distribution lines are the branches, and the spray heads are the leaves.

Now it's time to work on the branches. Let's say you've figured out how much pipe you want to get—you've paced off or measured the distances, or used an architect's scale to make that determination. You next need to decide what kind of pipe to get.

Buying PVC Pipe

When it comes to pipe, there are only four basic questions to ask yourself:
• What kind?
• How thick?
• How long?
• What flow diameter?

In chapter 1 we discussed the relative merits and uses of copper, galvanized, and PVC pipe. If you've completed the mounting of the valves on the manifold, you'll be working in plastic from here on out, so let's talk PVC.

PIPE SCHEDULES
Pipes made from PVC plastic normally come in several schedules or classes, such as 200, 80, and 40, to name three of the most common. Bear in mind that the larger the schedule

number, the thinner the wall of the pipe will be. Thinner-walled pipe has the advantage of being cheaper and carrying slightly more water. Because its walls are so thin, however, Schedule 200 is almost like eggshell, and breaks very easily. Hitting Class 200 pipe with a shovel almost always results in cracking or shattering.

We recommend using Schedule 40, despite its greater expense and slightly reduced water-flow capacity. You can hit Schedule 40 with a shovel—hard—and it will resist breaking and cracking. It's also more resistant to freeze-fracturing.

Schedule 40 is not indestructible, however. Once, doing a retrofit, we whacked away with the mattock end of a pickax at what we thought was a root, only to find that the "root" was a length of Class 40 PVC that we'd managed to break in half. Fortunately, it's fairly easy to trouble-shoot broken PVC: Just clean up the break by snipping out the broken section with a pair of pipe cutters, then glue in a coupler, or a length of pipe and couplers if necessary, to reconnect the broken line.

Once you've decided on the wall thickness of pipe, you need to decide what lengths to buy.

PIPE LENGTHS
For irrigation purposes, pipe is most commonly sold in 10-ft. and 20-ft. lengths. The advantage of 10-ft. lengths, especially in larger numbers, is that they will fit into a pickup, or onto the roof of a sedan or wagon, better than 20-ft. lengths will. The disadvantage of using 10-ft. lengths on long, straight runs is that you'll have to glue in that many more straight couplers, or glue that many more slip ends to flared ends. The bigger the site to be irrigated, the more of an issue this becomes.

For most smaller urban and suburban jobs, 10-ft. lengths can be more convenient. For larger scale jobs—athletic fields, estates, farms—20-ft. lengths are the way to go, especially if you have a rack or truck to carry them. Make sure you cut yourself some slack: Figure in a 1-ft. overlap on 20-ft. lengths, and a 6-in. overlap on 10-ft. lengths. Buying an extra length or two usually doesn't hurt, either.

Now there's only one question left on your checklist: What diameter?

PIPE DIAMETERS
Why are there so many diameters of pipe? Because different irrigation applications require different flow rates and pressures—a pop-up sprinkler head needs higher pressures and flow rates than a dripper does—which in turn require assorted diameters of pipe.

Here we will focus primarily on ¾-in. and ½-in. internal diameters, for these are most commonly encountered in landscape irrigation jobs. Nearly everything covered here scales up to larger pipe sizes too, but remember to switch from fast-drying PVC cement to medium-body glues if you're working with pipes bigger than 2 in. in diameter.

Keeping up pressure and flow

For every size you go up in pipe diameter—changing from ½-in. pipe to ¾-in. pipe, say—you are roughly quadrupling your flow capacity and losing less pressure to friction. Higher pressures mean you can put more heads, or more powerful heads, on a single line; this allows maximum efficiency per valve. For all these reasons, it makes sense to stay in as large a size of pipe for as long as appropriate for your irrigation system, even to the point of oversizing—using bigger pipe than your flows and volumes require. Doing so will keep the pressure and flow rates up in your overall system. Larger pipe costs a bit more, and larger couplers are a bit more expensive, but we feel that the long-term benefits far outweigh the initial costs.

Most pop-up, shrub, and flat-spray heads are sized for ½-in. or ¾-in. attachments, through a female-threaded orifice in the base or on the side of the unit. Some golf course and athletic field spray units, which put out great blasts of water, are sized for attachment orifices up to 2 in. in diameter. For most domestic uses, however, ¾-in. pipe is more than big enough at the spray end. A ¾-in. line can pump enough pressure and flow to run a head with a 50-ft. throw—enough to cover a circle 100 ft. in diameter.

Oversizing pipe can also be a benefit if you're working off a hose bibb. You may recall that one of the disadvantages of coming off a hose bibb is that you're already working at a ½-in. diameter. This deficit can be alleviated somewhat if you

This 2-in.-to-1-in. reducing bushing (left) inserts into a 2-in. tee (right). An arrangement such as this can be used for oversize lines in larger landscapes, for maximum pressure and flow.

Here's the same 2-in. tee with the reducing bushing glued in.

immediately size back up to ¾-in. pipe. This can be done by using a reducing bushing in reverse and thus sizing up from ½-in. to ¾-in. pipe at the gate valve. This will allow you to do all your manifold valves in the ¾-in. size. So, although your pressure will be down because you're coming off a ½-in. hose bibb, you will be losing less further pressure than if you had done everything in ½-in. pipe.

Branching pipe for even coverage
Why reduce flow diameters at all? Say you have ¾-in. pipe capable of safely delivering 8 gpm at about 30 psi, and you need to run four spray heads, each of which needs 2 gpm and 30 psi. On first examination you might think, "Well, I should just keep it all on ¾-in. pipe and run the four heads in a straight line off the pipe," right?

Incorrect Irrigation: Running Four Heads off a Single Line (cross-section)

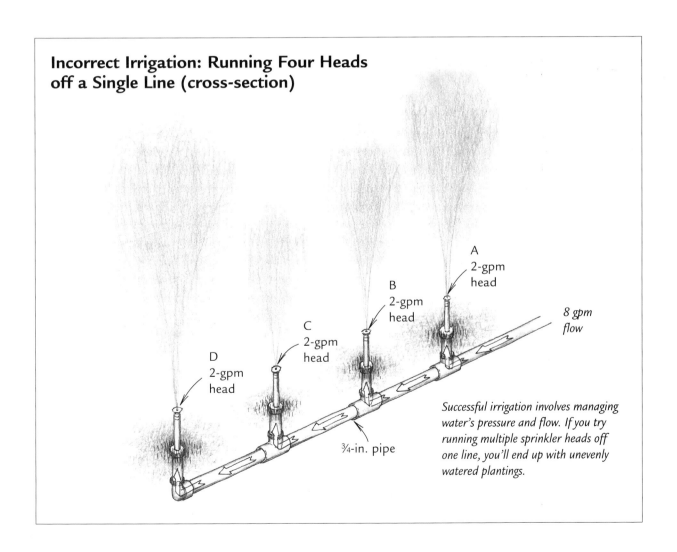

A
2-gpm head

B
2-gpm head

C
2-gpm head

D
2-gpm head

8 gpm flow

¾-in. pipe

Successful irrigation involves managing water's pressure and flow. If you try running multiple sprinkler heads off one line, you'll end up with unevenly watered plantings.

Wrong. Such an approach fails to take into account the physical properties of water. Run those four heads off a single line and what you get will look something like the situation in the drawing on p. 81. The sprays at points A and D will be high and strong, but the spray at B will be weaker, and the spray at C will be entirely inadequate. Why? Because you haven't taken into account that water has both pressure and flow.

Pressure means that water will try to escape through the nearest hole, point A. However, at point B and especially at point C, flow is working against pressure, which has already been reduced at A, so the water's momentum tends to move it onward rather than upward. What's happening at point D is known as hydraulic damming: Pressure and flow tend to push the water up, against gravity, at the last open point in the line.

A correctly branched line of four shrub-head sprinkler units.

This sort of improperly installed irrigation system results in the spotty dead pattern you can see in some irrigated lawns. You may have correct head-to-head spacing above ground, but without proper branching below ground you'll end up with uneven watering. To use that same example, the weak spray from the point C sprinkler head won't reach to points D or B, and the areas around those points will be underwatered. The grass around C will look fine because it's getting watered by B and D.

This same situation—8 gpm, 30 psi, four heads at 2 gpm each—can be addressed properly through lateral branching (see the drawing on the facing page). The ¾-in. pipe with 8 gpm comes into a ¾-in. tee, which divides the flow. There's a ¾-in.-to-½-in. reducing elbow on either end of the ¾-in. line coming out of the sides of the tee. Now you have 4 gpm coming through the outflow of that elbow. Because ½-in. pipe can safely run 4 gpm, you can now, from each elbow, run ½-in. pipe to a tee. From each of these secondary tees, you can run two pieces of ½-in. pipe, to ½-in.-slip-to-½-in.-male-threaded elbows. All you need to do is attach a ½-in. female-based 2-gpm sprinkler unit to each elbow. Voila! You have two sets of two sprinkler heads—four units at 2 gpm each, all spraying equally. This simple example of branching is laid out for you in the photo at left.

A final note on pipe diameter: In point of fact, a pipe has two commonly cited diameters: an inner diameter (the diameter of the hole in the pipe) and an outer diameter (that of the entire pipe, including the thickness of the pipe). Sometimes, particularly with poly hose and spaghetti line, manufacturers will only list the size, not specifying whether it's inner or outer diameter. Make sure to check the product specs. If you still can't find out the size, test the pieces before you buy them to make sure they fit together. Another solution is to stay with the same manufacturer so you don't end up stuck with fittings and pipes that don't fit.

How to Branch Lateral Pipes for Correct Four-Head Spacing

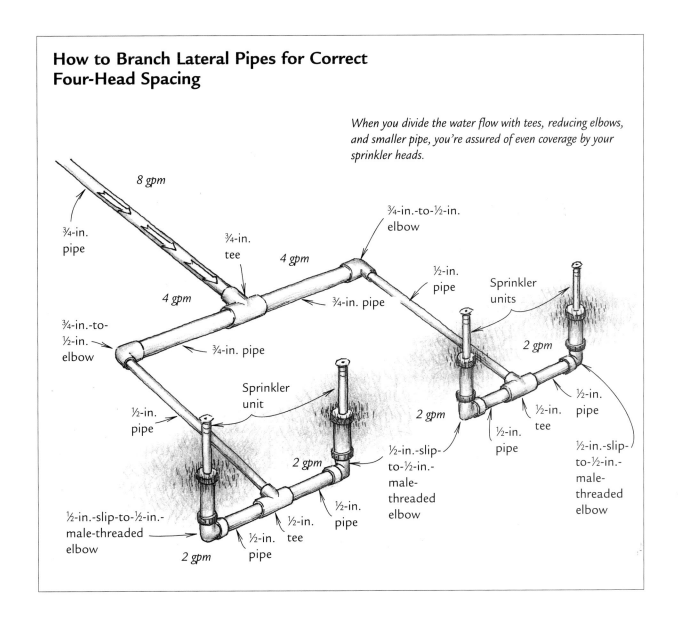

When you divide the water flow with tees, reducing elbows, and smaller pipe, you're assured of even coverage by your sprinkler heads.

8 gpm

¾-in. pipe

¾-in. tee

4 gpm

4 gpm

¾-in.-to-½-in. elbow

½-in. pipe

Sprinkler units

¾-in. pipe

¾-in.-to-½-in. elbow

¾-in. pipe

2 gpm

Sprinkler unit

½-in. pipe

½-in. pipe

2 gpm

2 gpm

½-in.-slip-to-½-in.-male-threaded elbow

½-in. tee

½-in. pipe

½-in.-slip-to-½-in.-male-threaded elbow

½-in. tee

½-in. pipe

½-in.-slip-to-½-in.-male-threaded elbow

½-in. tee

½-in. pipe

2 gpm

Learning about Linkages

At the hardware or irrigation store, you'll see bins and bins of parts and fittings. Don't give in to sensory overload. Relax. Walk up and down in front of the bins, reading the part description tags. Pretty soon you'll figure out where the ¾-in. parts are, and where the ½-in. parts are. Then you'll see that some parts are 1 in. on one end and ½ in. on the other; some go from ¾ in. to ½ in. Some go from threaded to slip, some from slip to slip. Don't worry about that just yet. Right now it's enough to get to know where the parts are. Each store does its parts inventory a little differently, so take the time to figure out your store's pattern.

Once you know where the different parts are, you need to think about what they're for. Basically, in the world of irrigation, everything slips together or screws together. In and of itself, PVC pipe only slips—it has no hose threads. If you want to give PVC pipe threads, you can use various fittings, such as a slip-to-thread adapter, to "graft" on threads.

Fittings have five major characteristics, which combine to build the universe of modern irrigation. Whenever you approach a part, keep these questions in mind:

- What material is it (PVC, Marlex, galvanized, brass, copper)?
- What species of fitting is it (elbow, tee, cross, reducer, bushing, straight coupler, nipple)?
- What size are its orifices?
- Are the orifices slip or threaded?
- Is the orifice threaded on the outside (male), or on the inside (female)?

Some of the nomenclature of pipework may still be confusing, so let's take a moment to explain it further.

REDUCERS

A reducer is any fitting—elbow, cross, tee, what have you—that helps you make the transition from one pipe diameter to another, or from one species of pipe to another.

For example, you must use a reducing fitting of some sort to go from ¾-in. PVC to ½-in. poly hose or soaker line. Switching to soaker or poly hose often involves a bushing—an adapter that is slipped *inside* the pipe (see the photos on p. 80). Switching to poly hose or soaker line involves not only changing to a different pipe diameter, but also changing from slip or screw fittings to compression fittings.

COMPRESSION FITTINGS

These fittings are usually slipped inside PVC pipe, then poly hose is slipped into them. In essence, compression fittings are a variety of slip fitting, but you have to work the poly hose or soaker line into the compression end,

Male Adapter

Male Adapter (Reducing)

twisting and pressing the hose until it won't pull out. The major difference between compression fittings and threaded or standard slip fittings is that with a compression fitting you don't need to use Teflon tape or glue. In the photo below, the compression fitting is the black piece between the poly hose and the elbow. It is about as close to brute-force jointure as we get in irrigation.

COUPLERS

A straight coupler or coupling is a cylinder used to join two pipes, with glue, threads, or, in the case of poly hose, brute force. Straight couplers are used not only to join lengths of pipe in initial construction, but also to troubleshoot broken pipe. In the latter case, you will usually have to cut off a bit of the broken pipe in order to "square up" the ends and allow room for the coupler to fit into place. (To "scab out" pipe refers to removing a section of pipe; to "scab in" pipe refers to inserting a coupler or small section of pipe.)

ELBOWS, CROSSES, AND TEES

In contrast to straight couplers, which simply join pipe, these fittings are used to shift the direction of the water flow and/or divide up that flow and send it in different directions. All three types of fittings are assemblages of 90° angles. The elbow, or ell, is a single 90° turn, the tee is two 90° angles, and the cross is four 90° angles. We have

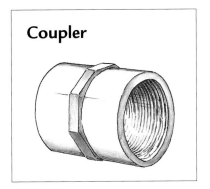

Coupler

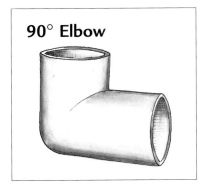

90° Elbow

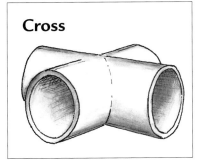

Cross

Tee

A ½-in. slip elbow and a compression fitting make the transition from ½-in. PVC to ½-in. poly hose.

A 4-in. endcap on a wellhead pipe end.

These odd-looking parts come in handy on some projects. Clockwise from top left: a braced elbow, a 45° elbow, a side-outlet elbow, a threaded plug, and an endcap.

also used Ys (three 90° angles) as well as the occasional angled fitting. Each type of fitting comes in myriad permutations and combinations, depending on the type of metal or plastic, and the type and size of orifices. Some of the more oddball parts you may encounter are shown in the photo above right. The photo above left shows an endcap for a 4-in. pipe wellhead.

Now you should be able to see that, despite all its apparent complexity, that wall of parts in the hardware store really only presents variations on a few simple themes. You're almost ready to go home and resume work on your irrigation system.

But let's take a moment first to discuss one of the most important irrigation tools you have at your disposal.

Using Tinkertoy Techniques

"Tinkertoy work" is the term we use for one of the most creative and innovative aspects of landscape irrigation. The Tinkertoy effect is usually seen at those locations in your system where you are altering some aspect of the water flow— changing its direction, dividing it up, or moving it from one size or type of pipe to another. Building a manifold is one example of Tinkertoy work. Mounting a spray head to a swing joint is another. These projects are the most complex pieces of Tinkertoy work that you are likely to encounter. If you can understand the geometry of swing joints and manifolds, and how to build them, there is no step in the design and installation of an irrigation system that you can't accomplish.

We use the word "Tinkertoy" because just as the childhood toy let you create what you liked from a few sticks and wheels, Tinkertoy irrigation techniques give you tremendous flexibility in building your irrigation system. All you need is a knowledge of what various parts can do.

Say you go to the hardware or irrigation parts store looking for a ¾-in.-slip-to-½-in.-threaded tee, but the store only has ¾-in.-slip-slip-slip tees. However, you see that the store also has ¾-in. slip-to-½-in. threaded bushings. If you've grasped basic Tinkertoy concepts, you know you can glue the slip-to-thread bushing into your slip-slip-slip tee and presto!—you've created the part you needed. It may have cost you 10 cents extra, but it's saved you from driving around to other stores searching for one elusive part.

Sometimes Tinkertoy work is not merely expedient but decidedly in the best interests of your irrigation system. On several jobs Tinkertoy techniques have allowed us to keep up ¾-in. pressure and flows all the way to where we teed off into poly hose: by taking a ¾-in. tee and fitting ¾-in.-to-½-in. bushings into it, then slipping ½-in. compression fittings for poly into the

You can buy prefabricated, lock-together manifold sections like these, but they lack the flexibility and adaptability of a custom-made manifold.

Building a Swing Joint

A movable swing joint is a valuable addition to your landscape irrigation system, providing complete articulation in three dimensions. Not only does a swing joint allow your sprinkler unit to "give" if someone steps or falls on it, it also allows you to move the sprinkler unit up or push it down if soil settling or plant growth change the ground level of your landscape.

Let's say you want to make a swing joint to connect ½-in. PVC pipe to a pop-up sprinkler unit with a ½-in. female-threaded orifice in its base. And let's say you want that particular sprinkler unit to come off the end of a run of pipe. How do you go about doing it?

First, because the unit is to come off the end of a run of pipe, you would use an elbow rather than a tee. Since you're attaching the swing joint and sprinkler unit to ½-in. PVC pipe, you know that one end of the elbow has to be ½-in. slip. However, the base of your sprinkler unit is not slip but a female-threaded orifice. What do you do?

The easiest solution would be to use a ½-in.-slip-to-½-in.-male-threaded elbow, or ell. That would work, but then your sprinkler unit would be inflexibly affixed to your pipe. For the flexibility of a swing joint, you should go with a ½-in.-slip-to-½-in.-female-threaded ell. All you need to turn the gap between those two female orifices into a swing joint are an 8-in. length of ½-in. nipple pipe and ½-in. Marlex street ells that are male-threaded on one side and female-threaded on the other (Marlex is a more flexible plastic than PVC; street ells get their name because they're handy for moving from street to household lines).

A Swing Joint in Three Dimensions

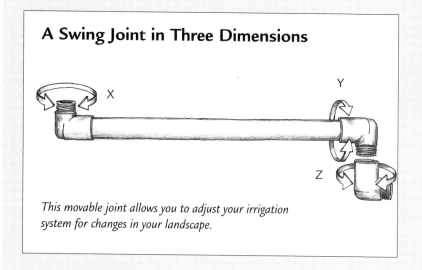

This movable joint allows you to adjust your irrigation system for changes in your landscape.

All a swing joint consists of are three Marlex street ells, a nipple, and geometry. Take two of the street ells and thread the male end of one into the female end of the other. You now have the initial pivoting unit, with a male end and a female end available for use. Screw one end of the nipple into the available female end of the two-piece pivot.

Now screw the female end of your remaining unattached Marlex street ell onto the available male thread of the nipple. Note that the swing joint is male-threaded on both ends. Screw one end of the apparatus into the female-threaded elbow orifice you earlier attached to the pipe, then screw the remaining male threads into the female-threaded orifice of your sprinkler unit. Presto! (The process is the same if you begin with a threaded tee instead of a threaded ell.)

Several manufacturers have recently started making and selling prefabricated swing joints and manifold sections. We do not recommend these because they are often less flexible than those you can construct for yourself at less cost. They also encourage you to be less flexible and self-reliant in your thinking about irrigation design and installation.

The basic components of the versatile swing joint: three Marlex street ells and a length of nipple with its male threads wrapped.

A swing joint for a pop-up sprinkler assembly. Note that both the tee and the sprinkler body base are female-threaded. The male-threaded ends of the swing joint screw into them.

A swing joint attached to a 12-in. pop-up allows for flexibility in several directions.

bushings' orifices (see the photo below). The photos on the facing page show various Tinkertoy combinations that can help you make the transition from ¾-in. PVC pipe to ½-in. poly hose.

Tinkertoy work saves you time and trouble by helping you create parts you can't find or don't have on hand. It expands the creation of an irrigation system beyond simple points and straight lines to planes (through arrays of horizontal and vertical pipe work) and ultimately, through swing joints, to three-dimensional space.

A transition via a slip bushing (white) and compression fitting (black).

With these points in mind, it's time to get started on the second leg of your irrigation system.

Working off the Manifold

Let's return to the point we left off on in Chapter 3, the manifold. You should be looking at a female-threaded outflow orifice on each of your manifold valves. If you'll be attaching PVC pipe of the same size, all you'll need for each valve station is a male-to-slip adapter in that size.

Start the first of your trenches leading out into the landscape from the manifold. You should dig a trench deep enough to hold two or three pipes, but you only need to start it—a 2-ft. to 3-ft. length of trench should do. For the moment, you just need to get a sense of how deep your trenchline is going to be, so you can see how long a piece of pipe you need to cut for the vertical (downward) piece coming off a given valve station on the manifold.

Thread a male-to-slip adapter into the female valve orifice. Measure off a section of pipe covering the distance from the valve's outflow orifice to the bottom of the trench. You can save yourself some time here by cutting the pipe to length and

From Pipe to Hose

These photos show different combinations for making the transition from ¾-in. PVC pipe to ½-in. poly hose.

Parts layout for making the transition from one ¾-in. pipeline to three ½-in. poly hose lines via a cross, three slip bushings, and three compression fittings.

This transition features (from bottom) a female-threaded tee, a male-threaded bushing, a male adapter, and a compression fitting.

This combination makes use of (from left) a ¾-in. slip-to-½-in.-thread reducing elbow, a ½-in. male adapter, and a compression fitting.

Yet another variation for transitioning from PVC pipe to poly hose, this time using (from bottom) a ¾-in. slip-to-thread elbow, a ¾-in.-to-½-in. reducing male adapter, and a compression fitting.

A six-station manifold built from galvanized and plastic parts. The three lines on the left have been fitted with slip-to-male-thread adapters. The three lines on the right have outflow pipes glued into place.

gluing a slip-to-slip elbow onto one end. This will become the bottom, or distal, end of the downward pipe section; it will eventually link up to the outgoing pipe.

Let's assume that the outflow end of the elbow is going to be directly in line with your trench. Glue the inside of the male-to-slip adapter and the outside of the near, or proximal, end of the pipe section, and insert the glued pipe into the adapter so that when you give the final, air-eliminating turn to the pipe, the outflow from the elbow at the bottom end will face down the trench in the direction you want the water to flow.

DOUBLING UP PIPES

If you don't want to dig any more trenches than you have to, you can save yourself some work at this point. You would be wise to double- or triple-up on the number of pipes per trench and run them parallel for as long as you reasonably can, especially if you're going to be trenching by hand and have more than a two-valve station manifold.

At this point it's easy to do. Let's say you have a valve station that is not directly in line with the outward-tending trench you've dug. Position the outflow elbow at the end of the downward pipe so that it is parallel to the manifold (see the top photo on the facing page). You only need to scab in a measured length of pipe to take you from that elbow to the nearest outward-tending trench. At that point you can glue on another elbow, and eventually run the pipe beside the other outward-tending pipes in the trench (see the bottom photo on the facing page).

This little parallel jog—from the bottom of your downward pipe, along the bottom of your manifold trench, to the outward-tending trench running to your plantings—costs you a little extra pipe and one extra elbow per station, but it can also save you a lot of shovel time.

PREPARING TO TRENCH

You're now looking at elbows into which you can slip your PVC. At this point go ahead and lay out the pipe pieces—unconnected—for all your lines along the entire length of the areas where you'll be laying pipe. Just to be on the safe side, allow yourself an extra 10 ft. of pipe per 100 ft. of trench. (Don't know exactly where to branch from one size of pipe to another? Reread the section on pipe diameters on pp. 79-83 and the poly hose section on pp. 99-102.) Mark out the lines of all your trenches with flags, string, or stakes.

Move the pipes aside and dig your trenches.

Trenching

Digging trenches with shovels is the most labor-intensive part of the job. If your landscape site is fairly flat, and you have the cash for it, you may want to rent a trenching machine. This can be worthwhile even on smaller properties, especially if you're likely to be encountering heavy clay or hardpan. On larger properties, we definitely recommend you make use of mechanical aids, including tractor attachments, Ditch Witches, Bobcats, and bulldozers that do trench work. You can rent a mechanical trencher for about $100 a day; most residential properties can be trenched out in a day or less if they've been prepped in advance.

However, if the landscape you're working on is steep, you may have no choice but to do the trenching work by hand. For

"Parallel jog" lets us avoid digging extra trenches. In this photo of a manifold trench, the elbows on the left have been turned parallel to the manifold.

A length of pipe has been scabbed in parallel to the manifold, then attached to a second elbow and a length of outflow pipe. Now the outflow pipes can go down the same trench.

Trenching in an unexpected snowstorm. Trenching machines make a hard job easier, if you're working on fairly flat land.

Poly hose of considerable length can be run off ¾-in. or ½-in. PVC, but be careful that pressures aren't so high that they burst the hose!

larger-scale irrigation projects, you may find that over-the-surface poly hose is a convenient alternative to pipe. Poly hose is especially helpful in terrain that's too rocky to trench through for burying ¾-in. or ½-in. PVC. Poly hose is flexible enough to wrap around surface rocks or be run along cracks in the rocks. Adapters let you make the transition from PVC to poly hose (see the photo at right above). This application is especially effective for larger-scale rock gardens, but it's also a good way to avoid trenching on steep slopes. Make sure you've taken steps to adapt your poly hose for pre-freeze draining by installing a drain plug at the point where the hose makes the transition to PVC.

Even in areas that do not suffer hard freezes, we recommend burying your PVC pipe 8 in. to 1 ft. down. In areas that do freeze, try to bury your PVC at least 6 in. below the average frost depth.

If you're using a mechanical trencher, don't go hog-wild with it and end up burying your pipes too deep. You'll have a difficult time uncovering them if you have to troubleshoot them later. In most areas of the contiguous United States, putting your irrigation pipes 1 ft. to 3 ft. down is deep enough.

Laying Pipe

When you've finished digging your trenches, bring the pipes up close to actual position again. Set out the pipes and all connectors—straight couplers,

Running Pipe under Pavement

Most residential irrigation jobs will require some placement of pipe under walkways, driveways, or other paving. Though this sounds like a challenge, it's actually quite easy, provided your soil is not rock or very solid hardpan, and the paved space is less than 20 ft. across. Just follow these steps:

1. Locate exactly where you want your pipe to go under the paving, and exactly where you want it to come out on the other side.

2. Trench at full depth all the way up to the paved space you wish to go under. Also trench a couple of ft. at full depth on the "exit" side of the pavement.

3. If you have a sledgehammer and a length of steel pipe slightly larger in diameter than the pipe you're going to be running under the paving, you can start your tunnel bore by laying the pipe in the trench and giving it a few good whacks with the sledgehammer. You only need a 3-ft. length of steel pipe to do this. We find that after about 1 ft., you've got a good bore hole started and can remove the steel pipe.

4. Take a length of PVC pipe that's a few ft. longer than the width of the pavement you're going under, and place it in the hole you've bored. At this point you can use water to soften the space you're digging through.

Attach a hose-threaded coupler to the back end of your pipe, and a hose, and turn the water on. If you've got good pressure and flow, there's no need to turn the water up full-blast. A moderate to strong flow will suffice.

5. Push your PVC pipe forward into the softening dirt beneath the paving. Slide the pipe back and forth from time to time. Be patient! This is a slow process, but it certainly beats the time and effort of ripping up your paving. Eventually the pipe will break through to the other side.

If your ground is too rocky or heavy to go through, or if you have to go more than 20 ft. (and therefore have to try to shove a coupler's outer diameter through the hole as well), you may want to consider renting a borer or hiring a contractor to do the tunnel for you. In the vast majority of situations, however, you can do it quite readily on your own, provided you're willing to be patient and don't mind getting a little muddy.

Using Water to Tunnel under Paving

By attaching a hose to your PVC pipe, you can soften the ground beneath the paving and work the pipe through.

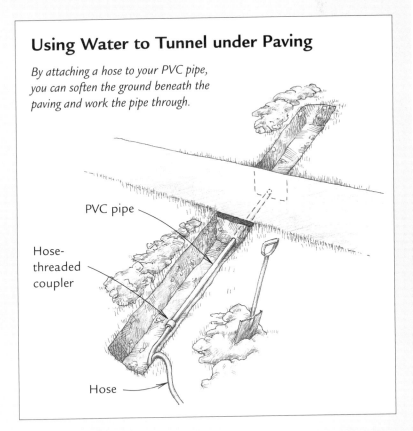

PVC pipe

Hose-threaded coupler

Hose

elbows, tees—wherever they'll be needed. Lay out all appropriate fittings for transitions from one size of pipe to another, from one type of pipe to another (from PVC to poly hose, for instance), and from your pipe to the sprinkler units and spray heads.

Warning! When you lay out your pipes, it's okay to see if parts fit into each other, but don't do hard mock-ups. If you do, you may find that you can't slip a fitting back off the pipe. Then you'll be tempted to glue all the other parts and leave the mocked-up piece unglued. Later, when you turn on the water, the unglued piece will pop off and you'll have a geyser of water, and all kinds of dirt in your system. Save yourself the trouble, and resist the temptation to do firm mock-ups.

At this point you should take the time to wrap all your threaded pieces with Teflon tape. Keep near at hand a box or bucket containing important spare parts. Make sure the lid on your glue can is loosened before you sit down to the work.

Do you remember flushing out your system after you got from the main line to the nexus for the manifold? You'll also need to flush out the system after you've attached the first lateral pipes. It's a smart idea to flush out each line each time you transition to a new pipe diameter. Don't worry if you build up some water in your trenches. You'll flush out the system for the last time when you're putting on the spray heads.

Now you're ready to piece it all together.

SIZING PIPE TO FIT

The phrase "sizing pipe to fit" is not the same as "sizing pipe." Sizing pipe means determining how much water can safely flow through a given diameter of pipe, referring to friction/pressure loss charts, and figuring out how much water your irrigation nozzle uses. When you size pipe to fit, you're coupling and linking lengths of pipe.

As you measure and cut pipe, it's best to remember two old carpenters' maxims. The first is, "Measure twice, cut once." The second is, "Measure and cut slightly long—you can always trim later." (Stu likes to stress the hazards of cutting short by joking, "Cut it short now—you can always glue pieces on later!") For most linkages, about 1 in. of pipe will be fitting into any given slip orifice, so keep that in mind as you measure your pipe for fit.

Measuring and cutting PVC pipe to fit is not rocket science. You won't need a compass, pro-tractor, or, usually, even a tape measure. Most measuring simply involves eyeballing a pipe length, then making a notch or line at the point where you wish to cut

Here's a parts layout for a lateral run of pipe. From bottom: ¾-in. pipe with a threaded tee, a ¾-in.-to-½-in. reducing adapter, ½-in. pipe, a ½-in. slip-to-thread elbow, a ½-in. threaded nipple riser, a pop-up sprinkler unit.

the pipe. PVC is a fairly forgiving material that will bend to fit without breaking (within reason, of course).

CUTTING PIPE

Cutting PVC is a good deal easier than going at galvanized pipe with oil and a hacksaw. A number of tools will cut PVC. The most common are saws and PVC pipe cutters, but even nylon string can saw through PVC if you've got the working room and the patience. The advantage of a hacksaw or coping saw is that you're more likely to own one than you are to own specialized PVC cutters, and you'll need one anyway if you're cutting into a household water line. However, saws require more space for their use, they are slightly more dangerous than PVC cutters, and they leave shavings in the pipe that can

Using PVC Pipe Cutters

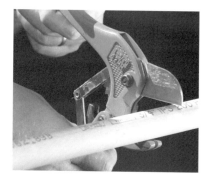

This pipe cutter is specifically designed to cut PVC. Note the ratcheting mechanism and "parrot beak" effect.

The cutting blade ratchets down into the pipe.

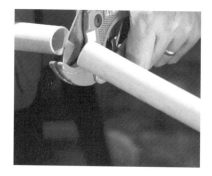

A clean cut.

clog your system and its heads. (You can greatly reduce the shavings problem by abrading the inside of the cut pipe with sandpaper, or even with a small rock, but that's an extra step.) On the whole, PVC pipe cutters are the best tool for the job.

PVC pipe cutters are essentially a single blade scissors—a little guillotine on a ratcheting mechanism. Because of the ratcheting mechanism, you can bring a considerable amount of force to bear on the blade even if you don't have Superman's handgrip. PVC pipe cutters are easier to use than saws, and you can maneuver with them more easily in tight work spaces—a big plus if you have to troubleshoot broken pipe. The disadvantages to PVC cutters are that the blades tend to break and the ratchets tend to wear out, unless you buy a fairly expensive pair.

GLUING PIPE

As you may have noticed from the photos in this book, PVC glue is messy—but also effective, since it is actually a solvent that melds the pipe and the fitting into one piece. For most applications, you'll be working with a quick-setting, light-bodied PVC cement that firms up in under a minute. For pipes greater than 2 in. in diameter, however, you'll have to make use of primers and heavier-bodied cements, which take longer to firm up.

Gluing PVC pipe that is 2 in. or less in diameter is an easy process. All you have to do to prep the PVC is clean off the area you'll be gluing. When you glue PVC, you usually have to glue only the outside of the first inch of pipe and the inside of the first inch of the fitting. For both surfaces, apply glue all the way around the circle. Then insert the pipe and quickly give the pipe and fitting a quarter-turn twist to eliminate air bubbles and potential hairline leaks.

In general, you will glue the outside of the slip pipe and the inside of the slip fitting. One of the few exceptions to this rule is found in the case of bushings. As stated earlier, a bushing is an adapter that allows the joining of pipes of different diameters by being slipped inside the pipe (see the photos on p. 80). In the case of slip bushings, you glue the inside of the pipe and the outside of the fitting. Threaded and slip bushings, along with bell reducers, are primarily of use in Tinkertoy situations.

Make the gluing process as easy on yourself as you can. Gluing is inherently messy, so don't worry too much about the occasional drip. You may want to lay a short length of pipe crosswise on, or in, the trench to prop up the pipe and parts you're gluing. This will help keep them out of the dirt and/or water at the bottom of the trench. Remember, if you do it right the first time, you won't have to replace it later.

Now we're ready to move out of the underground to the surface and near sub-surface.

Working with Hose

If your irrigation system includes microspray, in-line drippers, or soaker line, you'll be working with hose. Poly hose, "funny pipe," and black spaghetti are flexible and strong conduits that carry water from your PVC pipe to your spray heads. They allow you to extend greatly the branching of your irrigation "tree." Poly hose and, especially, black spaghetti lines are intended to be run along the surface or buried at a shallow depth in the near sub-surface.

All three types of hose are made from polyethylene and vary only in wall thickness and hole diameter. Increasingly, the lines between the types of hose are blurring; manufacturers now are producing ¼-in. poly hose.

POLY HOSE

Poly hose is an impressive and highly adaptable technology that in appropriate contexts can save you much travail with trenching shovels and glue. Numerous standard sprinkler heads,

including shrub heads and pop-ups, as well as stream rotor and single-stream gear-driven heads, can be attached directly to poly hose without warping or bursting the hose. You just need to take care to stay well below bursting pressure. The resistance of poly hose to UV damage is another plus for a distribution mode that works best running across the surface.

Poly hose has a few underground uses, too. For a quick spray head retrofit to an existing irrigation system, you can pop out the old heads on their pipes, run poly hose from the pipe location to your new spray head placement, and install the new head to the poly hose.

The fact that poly hose is linked together with compression fittings rather than threaded or glued fittings makes for easy installation and repair. We recommend push-in compression fittings instead of slip-over fittings in most applications (see the photo on p. 100), because the line pressure increases the snugness of the fit.

The fact that poly hose generally runs across the surface means that it's usually not appropriate for areas that will be mown. Also, its non-rigidity can be a problem. Although poly hose comes in diameters of up to 1 in., it is usually sold in the

These three poly hose lines are ready to be pushed into a compression tee.

½-in. size. You can't run ½-in. poly vertically (as to a manifold or an elevated shrub head) and put any sort of weight on it without staking it. (The staked shrub-head stream rotor on p. 11 is connected to poly hose.) PVC generally works much better in such vertical, weight-bearing situations.

Also, it's easy to puncture poly hose, and this can be a problem when you're digging around in your landscape. One solid hit with a shovel will cut a poly hose line straight through, and then it's time to run for the compression couplers to make it whole again.

"FUNNY PIPE"

There are a number of trade names for thick-walled poly hose, "funny pipe" being one of the more common. This heavy hose offers greater rigidity and resistance to bursting than standard poly hose, as well as larger diameters. However, "funny pipe" is no more resistant to animal-chewing, and it is considerably more expensive than standard poly hose, which is sufficiently resistant to bursting at most available domestic pressures and flows.

Another difficulty of thick-walled poly hose is that it is manufactured for use with special fittings and hose clamps. Standard poly hose can be easily worked into compression fittings that require no hose clamps or additional parts.

Quite a large number of sprinkler delivery types can be directly mounted to thick-walled poly hose, making "funny pipe" a popular, flexible alternative to building a swing joint. A Tinkertoy swing joint, however, provides fuller articulation in more directions than a "funny" joint does.

BLACK SPAGHETTI

We use the generic term black spaghetti because different manufacturers of this ¼-in. distribution tubing have different names for it: bubbler tubing, microspray tubing, and dripper tubing, to name three. There is even ⅛-in. distribution line for use with micro-flappers, which are used to water in very tight places. Essentially this thin line is just a stepped-down version of ½-in. poly hose.

Spaghetti line is polyethylene line, offering all the advantages of flexibility, UV resistance, and the like that you find in ½-in. poly. However, the small diameter of spaghetti line means that all of the applications coming off the tubing are micro applications—forget about water guns when you're working in this stuff!

Spaghetti line's disadvantages are much the same as those of ½-in. poly hose. Because of the way it attaches to ½-in. poly and its use in microspray with lower pressures and flows, ¼-in. and ⅛-in. black spaghetti are more

prone to clogging than larger capacity lines are.

FITTINGS

The last time you'll use glue or thread on any given irrigation line is when you are attaching a sprinkler unit orifice, or an adapter for such an orifice, to PVC, or when you're attaching a poly hose compression fitting to PVC. Once you're in poly, it's all compression fittings.

Thick-walled "funny pipe" usually attaches to PVC through male thread on both ends— much as you would expect a stripped-down version of a swing joint to do. The diversity of ells, tees, crosses, and straight couplers that we saw in PVC fittings also exists for compression fittings, except that you don't have to worry about slip or thread, male or female. The only choice is between push-in or slip-over attachment options.

Once you're in ¼-in. or ⅛-in. distribution line, things simplify even further. Though you still find fittings shaped like elbows, tees, and straight cylinders, they are now called barbs (elbow barbs, straight barbs, etc.). Barbs can only go *into* pipe—they are all slip-over, in other words.

Black spaghetti line most commonly attaches directly to ½-in. poly hose through puncture. You can buy a small hole punch "key" at most irrigation and supply stores; it's made specifically for punching holes in poly hose. Punch a hole at the appropriate point along the ½-in. line, and insert a barb—usually an elbow or straight barb. Over the free end of this barb, you slip one end of a measured length of ¼-in. distribution line (which we will focus on, since it's much more common than ⅛-in. line). The other end of the distribution line slips over the inflow orifice of a riser, dripper, or bubbler (see p. 14)—putting you, finally, at the spraying end of a micro irrigation line.

If, years down the road, you find yourself troubleshooting your system and you're out of barbs, and you've misplaced your hole punch key, you can use the point of a ball point pen to punch a hole in ½-in. poly hose. If you quickly insert an end of ¼-in. black spaghetti line into the fresh puncture, you will find that the ½-in. hose will reseal to a certain degree, enough to lock the ¼-in. line in place without need of a barb.

This is definite brute-force jointure, however, and we don't recommend that you make it your standard operating procedure. It increases the likelihood of small gaps that can leak and attract small slugs, insects, and worms. If the creatures die inside your pipes, they can clog your microspray or bubbler heads. There are few troubleshooting tasks less pleasant than trying to blow or suck a microspray head clean—especially when the culprit is a dead insect.

Black spaghetti lines are the final laterals, the ends of your "tree" branches. Next come the "leaves," the sprinkler heads, where water comes into the light and air again after its long journey through the pipes.

CHAPTER 5

The End of the Line: Water Meets the Yard

If you're like us, this is the part you've been waiting for. You've flushed out your pipes and you're eager to install your sprinkler heads. We gave an overview of macro and micro irrigation systems in Chapter 1. Now it's time to discuss sprinkler heads in more detail.

A quick note before we begin. Don't hesitate to pick up a brochure or product design manual for any of these products from the companies that make them—and read it. Each manufacturer has endowed its product with specific quirks or characteristics (using inner diameter as opposed to outer diameter fittings, for instance) that you would do well to familiarize yourself with.

Sprinkler Heads

We'll start with the most precise micro sprinkler systems, and then work our way up through the macros.

SOAKER HOSE

Soaker hose is a technology that keeps getting better and better. If we may continue with our tree analogy, soaker hose is a branch that gives off water like a leaf. It's unique in that it's a small-orifice, "low and slow" application that comes directly off larger lateral "branches."

As we mentioned earlier, soaker hose is particularly appropriate for watering roses, shrubs, and hedgelines, and inappropriate for areas that tend to be mown and flat, such as lawns (see pp. 18-19). Microflooding soaker line allows you to water less on steeper slopes and achieve the

A busy and efficient soaker hose junction. A ½-in. poly hose line comes into a male-threaded compression tee (a specialty fitting). Soaker hose from another line passes under the tee, ensuring that even the junction area is watered.

A soaker hose in "J loop" formation, with glossy black poly lines, a specialty tee, and a length of matte black soaker hose. (The "stick" inside the circle is newly planted dormant grape vine.)

The end of a soaker hose line, featuring a female-threaded endcap and a coupler that's male-threaded on the outside and compression on the inside.

You'll need these parts for a four-line bubbler. Left to right: an elbow, a nipple riser, and a bubbler junction surrounded by four lengths of spaghetti line.

The four-line bubbler is assembled and ready for duty watering a group of four large tomato plants.

"slow rain" effect on hillsides— a particularly appropriate use for it. Regulating soaker line pressure can be especially important on slopes, however, so making your own regulator is a good trick to learn (see p. 19).

Soaker hose is found most commonly in 100-ft. rolls of ½-in.-diameter tubing. It's a very ecologically sound product: an efficient watering system that helps recycle a big waste problem, used tires.

Although soaker hose is clog-resistant, if you live in an area with extremely hard water, your hose eventually will be blocked by mineral deposits. You can clean out the hose with a solution of water and vinegar, but this can be a bit of a nuisance. Even if you don't put filters or flow regulators on your other lines, it might be worth your while to put them on soaker line.

DRIP SYSTEMS

Drip systems work well for any application where you have a need for distributed spot flooding (hedge bases, fruit trees, shrubs). Also, any delivery system whose flow rate at each head is usually listed in gallons per *hour* has an important future as water conservation becomes more and more of an issue.

Drip covers a wide variety of systems—from disposable "T tape" (something of a cross between ⅛-in. spaghetti line and soaker hose) that's used in irrigated strawberry fields, to bubblers on the ends of ¼-in. distribution tubing, to drip units plugged directly into the walls of ½-in. poly hose (see the photo on p. 14). All these systems are essentially low-pressure, slow-flow leakers that deliver water directly to the base of a plant (see p. 10).

There is a down side to drip systems. Their relative permanence as surface-level features makes it hard to mow or harvest around them, and if you are in a very rural setting you may find that the local critters like to chew on your drip lines.

Drippers' "low and slow" efficiency is directly related to their tendency to clog with particulates or hard minerals in

Here is the parts layout for an eight-line bubbler...

the water—a real consideration if you're going to be working off a well. Their slow flow rates mean that some sort of pressure regulation is necessary.

On the plus side, you can control pressure from the output end by putting the appropriate number of bubblers, leakers, or drippers on the line; simply multiply the number of heads you wish to put on a line by the flow rate per head. Most drippers, bubblers, and leakers are also easy to clean and troubleshoot.

MICROSPRAY

Microspray heads are great for watering large beds around a lawn, as long as you don't stick them in the lawn, where they can get cut by mowers. They're great for filling in those tough-to-irrigate spaces where conventional spray heads throw too wide, and drip or soaker is too narrow. Microspray remains a specialty irrigation system,

...and here's that bubbler assembled, featuring eight lengths of spaghetti line.

The parts layout for a basic shrub head is simple (from bottom): a threaded tee, a nipple, and a shrub head.

it's a fairly inexpensive way to get into more specialized irrigation, though you will probably have to buy a lot of heads.

Microspray is in its own way a transition technology between line and spot flooding, and broadcast spraying. It retains much of the efficiency of low and slow irrigation, while providing the wider coverage of broadcast spraying.

Microspray takes us, for the first time, into spray coverage arcs. Spray arcs are based on a full circle. Thus, a 90° arc is a quarter, 120° is a third, 180° is a half, 240° is two-thirds, and 360° is a full or whole. See p. 8 for a photo of a 90° microspray head in operation.

Components

Most microspray units have three components: a spike, a riser, and a spray head (see the photo on p. 18). Distribution line (usually ¼ in.) attaches to a slip-over inflow orifice, which is molded into the spike. The outflow orifice, at the top of the spike, is inserted into a riser (usually another piece of tubing). A spray head is inserted at the top of the riser. The spray head may be a single body or consist of two parts—a pinhole orifice and a cap that shapes and directs the spray. Because they are mounted on stationary risers, most microsprays are technically "shrub" heads (in contrast to those on mobile internal lifting

however, largely because it is best adapted to gardens and flower beds—and for better or worse, lawns still make up the lion's share of the landscaped surface area in North America.

Advantages

It's possible to do entire landscapes in microspray. This is a particularly appropriate application in a square of new garden or a large bed dense with bulbs and perennials. In these cases, soaker hose "line" watering and drip "spot" watering will not work nearly as well. Microspray is also very cheap per sprinkler unit, so apparatuses, known as "pop-ups"). For the layout of these parts, see p. 22.

We prefer the two-part spray head because it is a bit easier to clean—simply pop off the cap and invert the spray orifice to flush it out—even if its individual parts are smaller and easier to lose. Single-body spray heads usually have to be reamed out with a short length of thin wire (a stripped twist-tie will work). Why worry so much about cleaning them? Because they will get dirty and clog, sometimes even clogging with decomposed insects at the point where the ¼-in. tubing hooks into the ½-in. poly hose.

Drawbacks

As with drip systems, microspray's big drawbacks are its permanent presence above ground, its tendency to clog, and its need for pressure regulation. Microspray is not appropriate for areas that will be mown or harvested near ground level. We have also found that children, dogs, and cats often knock off the risers. It's relatively easy to troubleshoot misplaced risers and clogged microspray heads, but it can be an ongoing annoyance.

SHRUB HEADS

The basic shrub sprinkler head is mounted on a permanent riser, typically 1 ft. to 2 ft. above ground level. For many people, these inexpensive flat-spray heads are a popular alternative to pop-ups. They work well in low-growing perennial beds.

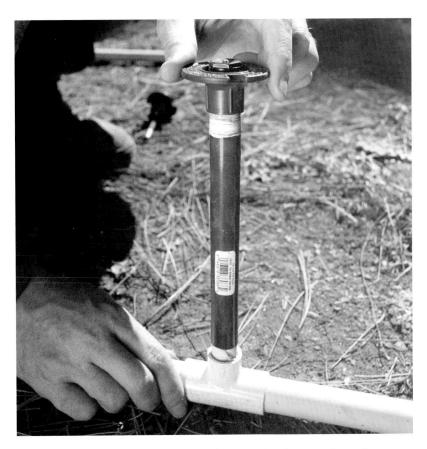

To mount a basic shrub head to an in-line tee, simply screw the male-threaded nipple into the tee.

CONVENTIONAL POP-UPS

Pop-up heads are the most popular irrigation method. They make a lot of sense for lawns, athletic fields, and golf courses. In these areas, you want to be able to mow without running into sprinkler heads all the time.

Components

A conventional pop-up—also called a lawn head—usually has a female-threaded orifice in its base, and attaches to a male-threaded nipple that's used as a riser. The riser is usually screwed into the female-threaded outlet of a tee or ell, which in turn is

Here's a basic shrub head, mounted.

Two pop-up, or lawn head, spray assemblies. The spray nozzles and their debris screens are in the foreground. The 6-in. pop-up unit on the right is in the deployed position. To its left, a 12-in. pop-up unit is uncapped and disassembled—note the spring-loaded mechanism.

This pop-up water gun is mounted directly on an elbow. Most of this unit will be invisible.

A pop-up water gun in the deployed position, mounted to a tee on a ¾-in. line. In operation, the line, riser, and sprinkler body all will be buried. Only the deployed lifter will be visible when the unit is operating.

slip-glued to a lateral, or "branch." In contrast to the riser seen in microspray, this nipple riser does not break surface. Rather, it is used only to prop the assembly so that the top of the pop-up head is even with the grade of the lawn. Given sufficient water pressure, the spray orifice (mounted on a short length of pipe or tubing) pops above grade and sprays. When the water pressure is cut off, the spray orifice falls back into the body of the spray unit, below the grass, so that mowing and other lawn activity present no hazards.

Drawbacks

Unfortunately, the simple and seemingly perfect pop-up system must function in an imperfect world. Most of the problems with pop-ups involve the issue of grade. The rigid connection of the head to the pipe means that if the placement of the top of the head is even the slightest bit off, there will be problems. A head that is significantly above grade after the ground settles can be tripped over or hit by the blades of a lawn mower.

A more common problem is that the top of the head ends up below grade, either because of errors in installation or because the grade changes over the years as the lawn grows in. This can result in a muddy environment for the pop-up to try to function in. Many of these sprinkler heads have a small wiper blade that keeps the pop-up tube clean so it can deploy fully, but sometimes the wiper gets grit in it. The pop-up locks up and shoots water at odd angles from the body of the unit. Nine times out of 10, this problem is caused by a clog-induced failure to deploy properly.

Swing joints

We recommend that you mount your pop-up spray unit on a swing joint instead of rigidly attaching it to the pipe. The spray unit will be easier to pull up or push down to grade as the need arises (see pp. 88-89).

Swing-joint mountings can also be helpful in other grade-dependent applications.

Most of the spray heads we talk about below—modifieds, stream rotors, impact heads, water guns—can also be mounted to pipe laterals in the fashion we have just discussed: either rigidly mounted via a male-threaded nipple, or swing-jointed. Allowing for bursting pressure, one can also mount most of these spray units on poly hose, using compression fittings and slip-to-male adapters.

Made from a nipple and two Marlex street ells, this swing joint (top) will provide extra flexibility for this 6-in. pop-up head.

Nipples of various types, threadings, and sizes. One of their many important uses is as connectors between buried pipe and sprinkler units that pop up and deploy at the surface.

If you decide against building a swing joint, here's the parts layout for mounting a pop-up head directly to a water line. From bottom: a ¾-in.-to-½-in. reducing elbow, a nipple, and two Orbit pop-ups (the top one is in the deployed position).

Here's another layout for mounting a conventional pop-up on a branching lateral. You just need an elbow, a nipple, and a pop-up. This basic approach holds for most pipe lengths and most types of pop-up heads.

Two pop-ups, mounted on lateral pipes.

Conventional pop-ups come in a fascinating array of models and styles, all varying in technological sophistication and cost. On the whole, they remain simple and cheap. Most conventional pop-up heads require fairly high pressure and flow, and they are often water-intensive (especially when poorly maintained). This higher flow often means runoff problems, particularly on steeper slopes and in looser soils. Some attempts have been made at making the conventional pop-up "lower and slower" and therefore more water-efficient. It is to these attempts that we now turn.

MODIFIED POP-UPS

Although pop-ups require a certain amount of pressure to operate, they don't necessarily need a high flow rate. Most attempts thus far have involved mounting smaller, microspray-type orifices on standard pop-up bodies (see p. 16). Such ongoing attempts to improve the efficiency of conventional pop-ups are laudable, but more work still needs to be done. Pop-ups with micro orifices are even more prone to clogging and "failure to deploy" than conventional pop-ups are. As a result, recent efforts toward improving the water efficiency of pop-up heads have moved away from spray and toward the stream. This change has been part of a larger movement away from simple static spray patterns, toward streams of water in carefully controlled motion.

Which brings us to stream rotors.

STREAM ROTORS

Stream rotors have been around in irrigation for more than 30 years, but only within the last 10 years has stream-rotor technology reached the point where it can compete with traditional flat and angled spray heads. Like flat and angled spray heads, stream rotors come in shrub (stationary riser) and pop-up (mobile lifter) variants. There are both multiple-stream rotors and single-stream rotors. For the moment, let's confine our discussion to the former.

Multiple-stream rotors, in both shrub and pop-up variants, combine some of the best characteristics of micro's low and slow water efficiency with the broadcast capabilities of macro sprays. Because they put down rotating streams, rotors apply water more slowly to the soil surface. This makes them more water-efficient than static sprays, and particularly appropriate for steeper slopes or the loosened soil of newly planted areas.

Multiple-stream rotor heads are usually sold as sealed bodies that are resistant to clogging and

This stream rotor head is mounted on a nipple that connects to an ell. The ½-in. pipe lateral connects back to a tee in the ¾-in. line.

stoppage by debris. Since they are gear-driven, they tend to be much quieter than impact heads. Stream rotors also tend to be less prone to lofting than sprays, so water loss to wind is reduced. Best of all is the aesthetic effect of their slowly whirling water streams, which resemble helicopter blades.

Like all shrub and pop-up heads, multiple-stream rotors should throw clearly—above obstacles—but should not be mounted so high that their effective coverage is reduced. This is particularly important for shrub heads, which are often mounted significantly above grade. The only major drawback we've found to multiple-stream rotor systems is their cost per spray head—$9 to $12 for most applications, though prices have been dropping. If you've got ample water pressure and big blocks of yard or garden to water, we find that these heads are worth the extra expense, saving you both maintenance costs and time.

IMPACT HEADS

More properly referred to as "impact-driven heads," impacts are an older technology that still sees a lot of use (see p. 15). Impacts also come in shrub and pop-up variants. They are cheaper and lower-tech than most stream rotors, but if you want to apply water steadily to a lot of flat space, you could do worse than impact heads. Some of these heads throw water more than 200 ft., irrigating a circle more than 400 ft. in diameter!

Not surprisingly, impacts work best in large-scale agricultural and ground cover applications, where they have a time-honored niche. Lately, some impacts have been re-engineered for greater water efficiency. Who says you can't teach an old technology new tricks?

Most impact heads are not particularly attractive in spray form, and they do tend to be noisy, producing that *chikchikchik* sound. However, if you have a lot of space and water, and are not too particular about how your system looks when it's in operation, impacts may be just what you're after.

WATER GUNS

Water guns are single-stream heads with at least ¾-in. female inlets and throw radii greater than 35 ft. For athletic field and golf course applications, we've come across water guns with 1-in. and even 2-in. inlets—a lot of flow to have at your disposal.

Gear-driven heads increasingly dominate the "long throw" market. The most popular of these are the single-stream rotor heads. These heads have all the advantages of the multiple-stream heads we covered earlier, but the big singles are not quite as attractive in spray form.

Water guns come in both shrub and pop-up variants, and can be mounted to pipe laterals in the variety of ways we described in the section on conventional pop-ups (see pp. 107-110). The manufacturers of these big heads are constantly trying to improve their water efficiency, but this is an uphill battle. It's hard to make "long throws" operate low and slow. In order to get the widest possible distance between heads, with full coverage from the base of the spray head to the farthest part of the throw, sprinklers require increasing amounts of pressure and flow. The longer the throw, the higher the pressure and the faster the flow required for full coverage.

Looking across the spectrum of broadcast spray irrigation, from microspray all the way up to the big impact heads and water guns, and even to wheeled sprinkler arrays and other agricultural uses (see p. 9), the pattern becomes clear: The more like a farm field the landscape is (big, flat, to be mown or harvested), the bigger spray radius per head it can take, and the greater pressure and flow it requires for full coverage.

Economies of scale kick in at larger-scale applications. Though big single-stream rotor and impact heads are far more expensive than microspray heads, fewer total heads are

A pop-up water gun with a ¾-in. orifice, mounted on a ¾-in. riser. The fitting and pipe are also ¾ in.

required for complete coverage of a given area. In all circumstances, the key thing to remember is to match the type of irrigation to the crop and landscape size, as well as to the expense and availability of your water. We will discuss this matching process more fully in Chapter 6. First, let's discuss how to automate your irrigation system, no matter what size sprinkler heads you decide to use.

Automating Landscape Irrigation

The automated sprinkler valve controller—more commonly known as a sprinkler controller or timer—is the robotic heartbeat of your irrigation system. It tells your irrigation system when, how long, and how often to water. It also tells your system which pipelines and spray heads to use.

When your clock ticks around to watering time and your digital or analog switches throw, a current of electricity travels from your timer through the line connect-ing your station termin-als to your control valves. Inside the valves, the electricity gener-ates a magnetic field that actu-ates the flow of water through the valves and into your pipes and to your spray heads. All this happens in the solenoid, which is attached to the top of your control valve and connected by wires to your timer.

THE SOLENOID

The solenoid acts as an electrical switch that works much the same way the toggle switch on your wall turns lights on and off. The solenoid features a little rod of metal that sits inside a coiled spring; an electrical cur-rent tells the rod to open and close the valve.

We're taking time to describe the inner workings of the solenoid because its parts—the coil and metal bar—are the pieces most commonly missing in defective automatic sprinkler valves of both the brass and the plastic varieties. Before you hook up your timer, we recommend that you detach the solenoid housing from each of your control valves—it's the part on the valve that the electrical wires trail out of, usually made of black plastic—and check to make sure that you can see a metal cylinder with a spring around it. If you do, screw the solenoid housing back on the valve. Do this for all the control valves on your manifold.

THE CONTROLLER

Controllers come in a variety of styles, shapes, types, and combinations of analog or digital

A six-station sprinkler valve manifold, under construction. Note the wires that will hook the solenoids of each valve to the time clock.

A nine-station time clock of mixed design—digital timing, analog switching. The faceplate has been removed to expose the clock's guts.

elements. Basically, they all function as switchboards. The real guts of the apparatus are usually discreetly covered by a removable panel. Beneath that panel, nearly all sprinkler controllers are characterized by a terminal strip—a metal strip with a row of Phillips-head screws going into it. Above each screw location there is usually a legend explaining (sometimes rather cryptically) what each screw-headed terminal is for (see the photo above). The most obvious are those screw heads affixed under numbers corresponding to the number of stations your timer offers. This is where you'll hook up the control wires from the solenoids of your valves to their respective stations in the timer.

You will also usually find a couple of screws labeled "A" and "B," sometimes under a legend marked "Common." This is a ground running to all your control valves. You will usually find a screw head with a "Pump" legend (if a main pump has to be activated for your sprinkler system), and screw heads with legends in volts, usually labeled 24V AC but sometimes ranging as high as 115 volts. These hook up to your power source. Often you will also need to install a 9-volt battery to supply power for a limited time in the event of a power outage. If your battery is weak or dead and your main power goes down, the clock time and watering times you've programmed can malfunction or be erased, shifting over to a default setting that may not suit the needs of your landscape.

You should mount your sprinkler controller in an accessible place, preferably where it won't be exposed to wet weather—unless, of course, it's contained in a waterproof box.

CONTROLLER HOOKUP

Wire cable usually comes bundled and sold as "part wire": five-part, eight-part, etc. Five-part wire, for example, has five different wires running through it. These are multicolored. For convenience and memory's sake, we designate the white wire as the "common ground" wire, and the remaining wires as the control wires. If you've got four control valves, you should be using at least five-part wire cable, so you have four control wires and one ground wire.

One wire from the solenoid in each valve connects to the white common ground line; the remaining control wire from each solenoid connects to one of the colored wires in your wire bundle. When hooking up electrical line from control valve solenoids to your timer stations, remember that at the timer end the white wire goes to ground and the colored wires go to the timer stations you've assigned to your control valves. Use wire

nuts augmented by latex fingernail polish, or grease caps, to protect your wire connections. (About the only time this scenario will change is if you're using "pigtail" wire, where the green line is the ground.)

You can run electrical cable any distance, but it's better to use continuous lengths in order to avoid weak connections. It's generally better not to splice wires together, if you can avoid it. The old carpenter's maxim applies to purchasing cable: Always buy long—you can trim later. Because you will be working with low voltages and very simple wiring, there's no need for you to hire an electrician to do this. Just buy the right wire and the right timer, carefully read the instructions, and you can get it done yourself.

CONTROLLER STATIONS

Control valves and sprinkler timers are not cheap, but the point is not to use as few of them as possible. Think of the different regions of your landscape—microclimates, shade and sun areas, wind factors, water infiltration versus runoff, slopes, even depths of solid substrate. These areas have different watering needs. The more control valves and timer stations you have, the more flexibly you can match your system to the variety of conditions in your landscape.

A four-valve manifold with hose bibb, all wired up to the timer shown on p. 115. After six years in operation, the manifold is still doing its job.

Setting program runs

When choosing a controller, ask yourself how much range in times it offers. Range in times is provided by what are known as program runs. Here's one example of how you can use them: Say you have an eight-station timer with two programs, A and B. You have five stations on A and three on B. Your A stations are areas you prefer to water in the evening, and the B stations are areas you want to water in the morning. You can set Program A to begin its watering cycle at 7:30 P.M. Program B can be set for 7 A.M.

It's nice to have at least two program runs, but three is even better. Let's say it's the middle of summer and you're putting a new lawn into an established landscape. You'll need to water that section more heavily than you do your established plants. If you've got a third program, you can set it to water the lawn section in the middle of the night. You can set it on Program A *and* Program C, and give the new lawn the extra moisture it needs.

Choosing a controller

At the hardware store, you'll see timers with buttons for their clocks and sliding toggles for their station controls. You'll see rotating dials marked with day and night cycles. Which timer is right for you?

Take into account the number of stations you'll need for your landscape, the number of program runs you think you'll need, and whether the controller comes with waterproof housing (which will determine where you mount it). After you've considered all this, pick up your chosen sprinkler controller, stand in the aisle, and read the instructions. If you can figure out how the timer works, that's the one for you.

If you are simply updating and automating an older manual valve sprinkler system, you will very likely have to replace the valves on the manifold if you want to go to a more fully automated sprinkler controller setup.

The Future and Its Possibilities

One can imagine a future irrigated landscape in which individual "leaves" of the irrigation "tree"—solar-powered, largely autonomous, incorporating tensiometers or neutron probes, computer chips, and radio links—will assess the condition of their environment, communicate with other "leaves" in the vicinity, and water as the need arises. With the development of new gel blocks that store considerable quantities of water in a biodegradable matrix, these end-of-the-line irrigation units will dole out water and nutrient-impregnated blocks as they "see fit," becoming almost completely autonomous, freed even of the constraint of pipes carrying liquid water.

Such scenarios are currently science fiction. Still, some of the newer technologies now coming on-line are pretty wild in themselves (see p. 23). Completely automated greenhouses, like computerized, tensiometer-driven irrigation, are already a part of the present.

The increasing application of technology to irrigation indicates a bright future—a place watered thoroughly yet efficiently. Such smart landscape irrigation will require smart installers and do-it-yourselfers. We hope that this book has been a step in that direction.

CHAPTER 6

Sample Irrigation Plans

In this section we're less concerned with providing specific designs than with providing the know-how for you to create your own design—and avoid common problems. Factors such as spray angles, psi, and pipe or distribution line diameters will vary depending on your situation, but the design principles will remain the same. Knowing these basic principles will help you adapt sprinkler coverage to any landscape space.

Spray Heads and Water Use Basics

Designing irrigation coverage is basically a matter of simple geometry—triangles, squares, and circles; radii, diameters, and arcs. Although the spray heads of more expensive systems are increasingly adjustable to a wide variety of angles, the vast majority of spray heads distribute water in only four types of arcs: 90°, 180°, 270°, and 360°, also known as quarter, half, two-third, and full arcs.

SQUARE SPACING

The plan on p. 120 provides a classic overhead image of how these angles are used to fill space—in this case, a 20-ft. by 20-ft. rectangle covered by what is known as head-to-head square spacing. Head-to-head spacing means that the farthest point of spray from any given head reaches the neighboring heads along its spray arc. Square spacing means that the space is covered or "filled" in terms of squares.

Head-to-Head Square Spacing: 20-ft. by 20-ft. Area

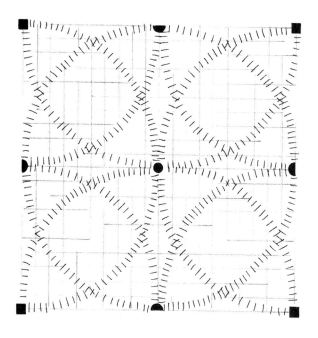

Key

■ 90° head ◗ 180° head ● 360° head |||| arc of spray

All spray heads have a 10-ft. throw radius.

How much water would such an array of sprinklers use? Let's say that these are all the same type of head and that, spraying in a 360° arc, one head uses 1 gpm. (The gpm, psi, and throw-distance data for your sprinkler heads can be found in catalogs from the manufacturer, on the packaging, and in the enclosed documentation.) Only one head out of the nine employs a full arc—the other heads fire off only fractions of that. A 90° head uses only one-quarter of the water that a full-circle spray head uses. In this case, each 90° head would use 0.25 gpm per head. Each 180° head uses half of what a full-circle head uses—0.5 gpm.

The equation to figure out the total water usage of this sprinkler array is thus:

$$1 \ (1 \text{ gpm}) + 4 \ (0.5 \text{ gpm}) + 4 \ (0.25 \text{ gpm}) = 1 \text{ gpm} + 2 \text{ gpm} + 1 \text{ gpm} = 4 \text{ gpm}$$

The large 20-ft. by 20-ft. square above breaks into four 10-ft. by 10-ft.-squares. Full head-to-head coverage of this space using sprinklers with 10-ft. throw patterns thus requires four 90° heads (one at each corner of the square), four 180° heads (one at the midpoint of each side), and one 360° head (in the exact center of the square). Nine heads, each with a 10-ft. throw radius, are used to cover 400 sq. ft.

Therefore, you must have a flow of at least 4 gpm to operate this group of sprinkler heads. If these are pop-ups that require a pressure of 35 psi to pop up and spray 10 ft., then you must have at least 4 gpm at 35 psi to operate the array we've sketched out here (check your sprinkler catalog, box, or documentation for psi).

The plan at right illustrates the same kind of head-to-head square coverage for a 10-ft. by 20-ft. rectangular bed. Here, 200 sq. ft. are covered by eight 5-ft. by 5-ft. squares. This time, however, let's hypothesize that our spray heads are a variety of efficient microspray that uses 0.1 gpm in a full arc of 360°. Each 180° spray head uses 0.05 gpm, and each 90° head uses 0.025 gpm. Applying our equation, we get:

$$3 (0.1 \text{ gpm}) + 8 (0.05 \text{ gpm}) + 4 (0.025) = 0.3 \text{ gpm} + 0.4 \text{ gpm} + 0.1 \text{ gpm} = 0.8 \text{ gpm}$$

Let's also say that you need 20 psi to get a full 5-ft. throw from each of these heads. If you have at least 0.8 gpm at 20 psi, you can operate this array of microsprays.

TRIANGULAR SPACING
Triangular head-to-head spacing can be used instead of square spacing. Although it's a less thorough form of coverage, triangular spacing may be appropriate for sparse or drought-tolerant plantings.

In the plan at right, we see a 400-sq.-ft. area covered by four triangles of 100 sq. ft. each. This coverage is accomplished using only five spray heads, as opposed to the nine heads used on the facing page. Let's assume that the 360° head at the center uses 1 gpm. Let's also assume that a head with a 20-ft. throw radius uses 2.8 gpm in full-circle operation, and that all our heads

Head-to-Head Square Spacing: 10-ft. by 20-ft. Area

Key
■ 90° head ◗ 180° head ● 360° head |||| arc of spray
All spray heads have a 5-ft. throw radius.

Head-to-Head Triangular Spacing: 20-ft. by 20-ft. Area

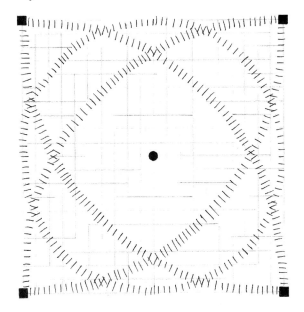

Key
■ 90° head ● 360° head |||| arc of spray
The 90° spray heads have a 20-ft. throw radius.
The 360° spray head has a 10-ft. radius.

operate at 35 psi. However, our four heads with the 20-ft. throw are only 90°, so each uses only one-quarter as much water as a full circle. Doing our calculation, we get:

$$1 \ (1 \ \text{gpm}) + 4 \ (0.7 \ \text{gpm}) =$$
$$1 \ \text{gpm} + 2.8 \ \text{gpm} = 3.8 \ \text{gpm}$$

The array shown in the bottom drawing on p. 121 will run on fewer total heads and lower overall gpm than the head-to-head coverage of the same space shown on p. 120.

CIRCULAR SPACING

It would be nice if the world were always as simple and straightforward as it is in the drawing below. This is as close to a Platonic ideal as one is likely to find in irrigation: a perfectly circular yard space that just happens to match the full-circle pattern of a spray head. This plan represents a circle 40 ft. across, with a 20-ft. radius. A 40-ft. by 40-ft. square would cover 1,600 sq. ft., but a 40-ft. circle covers only 1,256 sq. ft.

Nothing could be simpler to calculate than the irrigation needs of this circle—a single head, traveling a full circle, depositing 2.8 gpm of water. Unfortunately, in our imperfect world there would probably be a tree at the center of that circle, which would require other approaches.

OVERCOMING OBSTACLES

The plan on the facing page shows one way to water around an obstacle. (For a similar solution, see the drawing on p. 131.)

Using six of the same type of head that we used for the perfect circle—but with 120° spray arcs—we come to quite a different result. Each spray head uses only one-third as much water as a full circle, but since there are six, you'd need a minimum of 5.6 gpm to run the array, twice as much as you needed to run the "ideal" version at left.

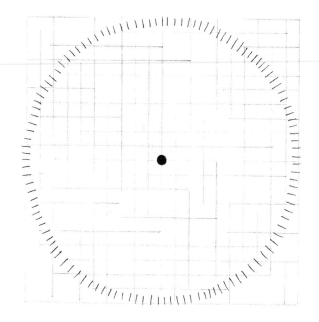

Single-Head Coverage: 40-ft.-Diameter Circle

Key
● 360° head |||| arc of spray
The spray head has a 20-ft. throw radius.

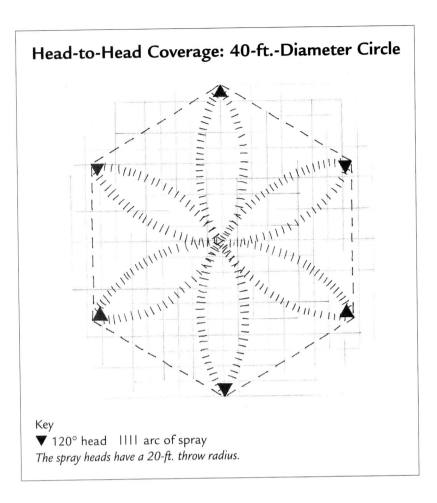

Head-to-Head Coverage: 40-ft.-Diameter Circle

Key
▼ 120° head |||| arc of spray
The spray heads have a 20-ft. throw radius.

There's a correlation between the number of spray heads and the amount of water used: The more spray heads, the more water they use. This brute fact means that the more fine-tuned your sprinkler coverage, the more complicated your water-use patterns become.

The problem we run into when we design irrigation for the real world is that the real world is neither geometrically regular nor free of obstacles. Say you have a flower bed shaped like the top drawing on p. 124: part square and part circle, rather like the key on a basketball court. Because this is a mixed figure, the far edge of the circle probably won't be watered as fully as the bottom of the square. Let's say we're once again using our pop-up heads from the drawing on p. 120, which throw 10 ft., use 1 gpm in a full circle, and require 35 psi. Calculating from the largest arc to the smallest, these heads use 2 gpm + 1.5 gpm + 1 gpm, or 4.5 gpm minimum.

Let's turn that space into a yard and stick a tree in the middle of the circle, as in the bottom

Coverage Options for a Square and Half-Circle

This 20-ft. by 20-ft. square and 10-ft. half-circle can be covered in several ways, depending on the obstacles involved.

All spray heads have a 10-ft. throw radius.

Combined Head-to-Head Square Spacing and Single-Head Coverage

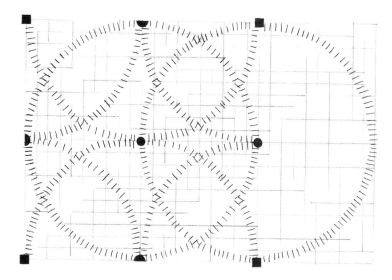

Key
- ■ 90° head
- ◗ 180° head
- ● 360° head
- |||| arc of spray

Combined Head-to-Head Square Spacing and Head-to-Head Full-Circle Coverage

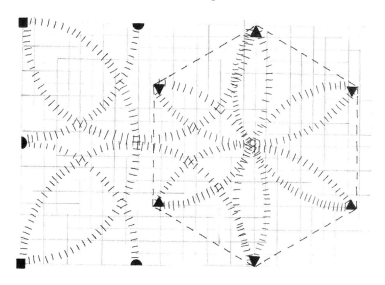

Key
- ■ 90° head
- ▼ 120° head
- ◗ 180° head
- |||| arc of spray

Combined Head-to-Head Square Spacing and Head-to-Head Half-Circle Coverage (I)

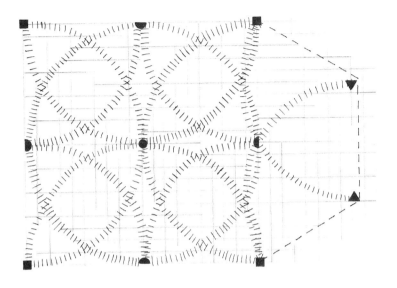

Key
■ 90° head
▼ 120° head
◗ 180° head
● 360° head
IIII arc of spray

Combined Head-to-Head Square Spacing and Head-to-Head Half-Circle Coverage (II)

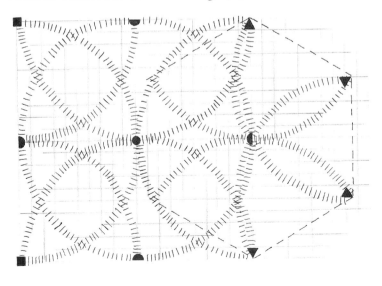

Key
■ 90° head
▼ 120° head
◗ 180° head
● 360° head
IIII arc of spray

drawing on p. 124. Calculating from the largest arc to the smallest, this array uses 2 gpm + 1.5 gpm + 0.5 gpm—still less than 4.5 gpm, but the coverage is even less thorough than in the previous example.

Now let's examine the plan in the top drawing on p. 125. Although this compromise uses the same total number of heads as the plan in the bottom drawing on p. 124, its water consumption is 1 gpm + 0.66 gpm + 2 gpm + 1 gpm—4.66 gpm. The slightly fuller coverage requires slightly greater water usage. The plan in the bottom drawing on p. 125 is another variation on the same theme. Calculating

from largest arc to smallest, we get water consumption of 1 gpm + 1.33 gpm + 2 gpm + 0.5 gpm, or 4.83 gpm.

Sectioning Irregular Spaces

Trying to cover an irregular space with spray arcs ends up distributing water very unevenly, as seen in the trapezoid below. What to do? The most common method is referred to as "sectioning" or "sectorializing." By turning a trapezoid into a rectangle and two triangles, as in the plan in the drawing on the facing page, you can maximize the regularity of sprinkler coverage. You're using the same number of heads and the same water flow, but more efficient head placement provides more even coverage. Note, however, that in both the sectioned and non-sectioned approaches there is still some overthrow from the units set to 180° on the long back side.

ESTABLISHING SECTIONS

The full value of sectioning as a space-filling technique can be seen in the plans in the drawings on pp. 128-129. Here we take an irregular "real world" landscape space and section it, turning it into rectangles, triangles, and arcs. The areas labeled Section 1 are to be planted in fescue grass, which is moderately drought-tolerant. The areas labeled Section 2 will form a long, L-shaped border, 6 ft. wide, of hardy, clumping perennials.

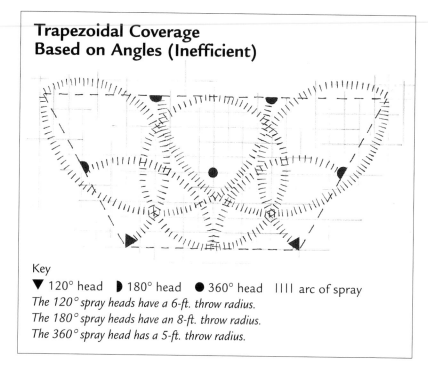

Trapezoidal Coverage
Based on Angles (Inefficient)

Key

▼ 120° head   ◗ 180° head   ● 360° head ||||| arc of spray

The 120° spray heads have a 6-ft. throw radius.
The 180° spray heads have an 8-ft. throw radius.
The 360° spray head has a 5-ft. throw radius.

Beyond the borders of Section 2 are drought-tolerant cedar and sugar pine woods that will not be irrigated. Because those woods are essentially fallow land, the slight overthrow at two of the corner areas of Section 2 will not pose a problem. In Sections 1 and 2, we're able to get by with slightly thinner coverage—that is, not full square spacing—because the plants are drought-tolerant.

In the area made up by Section 3, however, things are not so simple. The western edge of the space is bordered by a meandering tile path that we want to keep water-free. At the south edge of Section 3 is a garage and shed area, which we also don't want to spray. Section 3 will be planted in more tender annuals and perennials.

SELECTING SPRINKLERS

We have fairly common pressure and flow at this landscaping site—40 psi and 10 gpm. For the bigger area of Section 1, we decide to go with multiple-stream pop-up sprinklers that have a 42-ft. throw radius at 35 psi, and put out 3.6 gpm in full-circle mode. That means the single head set to 360° and the four heads set to 90° will use a total of 7.2 gpm. That gives us 2.8 gpm to play with. For each of the two smaller areas of Section 1, we opt for a standard fan-spray pop-up with a 12-ft. throw radius at 35 psi; it delivers 2.8 gpm in full-circle mode. Since we're only using two shrub

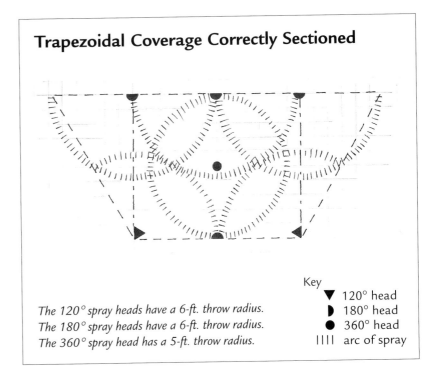

Trapezoidal Coverage Correctly Sectioned

The 120° spray heads have a 6-ft. throw radius.
The 180° spray heads have a 6-ft. throw radius.
The 360° spray head has a 5-ft. throw radius.

Key
▼ 120° head
▶ 180° head
● 360° head
|||| arc of spray

heads set to 90°, we will only use 1.4 gpm on the smaller areas. Thus we come in well below our available flow rate. By branching lateral pipes off a single valve, we could run this entire section off one station—provided we use 1-in. pipe to avoid pressure loss. This example indicates the value of oversizing pipe.

Pressure loss could be an issue in Section 2 as well. We decide to do this section in microspray (soaker would probably work equally well once the border plants are established). Let's say we use heads that throw 6 ft. at 4 psi, and deliver 0.25 gpm in full-circle mode. Most microspray heads throw farther and operate

A "Real World" Front Yard

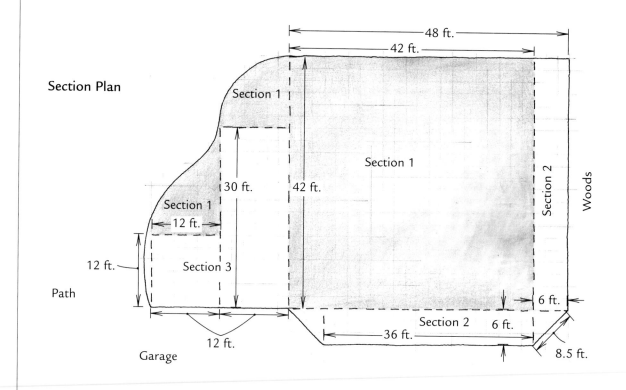

Section Plan

Section 1

Section 1

Section 1

Section 1

Section 2

Woods

Section 3

Section 2

Path

Garage

48 ft.

42 ft.

30 ft.

42 ft.

12 ft.

12 ft.

12 ft.

36 ft.

6 ft.

6 ft.

6 ft.

8.5 ft.

more efficiently at 10 psi to 20 psi, but we'll use this for the sake of example.

For our array of ten 90° heads and twenty-two 180° heads, we would get:

$$10 (0.0625 \text{ gpm}) + 22 (0.125) = 0.625 \text{ gpm} + 2.75 \text{ gpm} = 3.375 \text{ gpm}$$

This is well within our available flow parameters. For these beds, we could connect ½-in. poly hose to our PVC pipe underground, then run the poly along the surface, connecting our

distribution tubing and associated heads about every 6 ft.

From checking our psi loss charts, however, we see that for every 100 ft. that water travels at 10 gpm down ½-in. poly hose, there is a pressure loss due to friction of 34.67 psi! If we send our water down 85 ft. of ½-in. poly hose, plus distribution tubing, we'll be cutting it too close.

AVOIDING PRESSURE LOSS
There is a solution. We could stay in big pipe for as long as appropriate, then branch to

Coverage by Sections

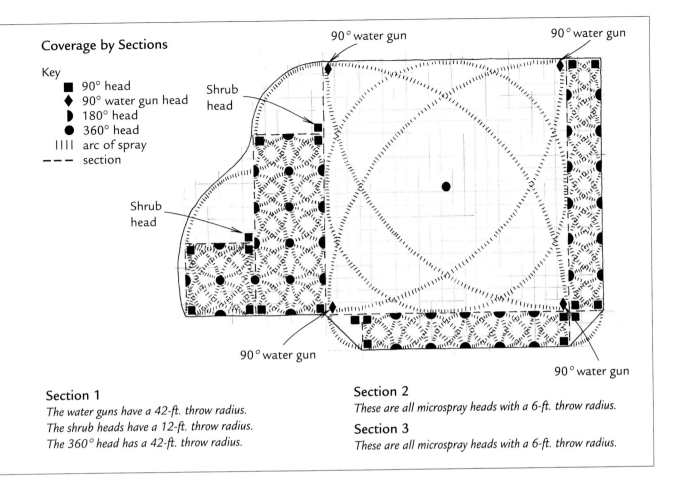

Key

- ■ 90° head
- ◆ 90° water gun head
- ◗ 180° head
- ● 360° head
- |||| arc of spray
- − − − section

90° water gun

90° water gun

Shrub head

Shrub head

90° water gun

90° water gun

Section 1
The water guns have a 42-ft. throw radius.
The shrub heads have a 12-ft. throw radius.
The 360° head has a 42-ft. throw radius.

Section 2
These are all microspray heads with a 6-ft. throw radius.

Section 3
These are all microspray heads with a 6-ft. throw radius.

accommodate, say, four 20-ft. lengths of poly hose. This entire array could be run off a single control valve and a single station, at closer to real-world pressures and throws.

We'd be a bit farther into the safe zone using the same sort of microspray heads—providing a 6-ft. throw at 4 psi and using 0.25 gpm in full-circle mode—in Section 3. Calculating from largest arc to smallest, we'd have:

$$5 \ (0.25 \ \text{gpm}) + 14 \ (0.125) + 8 \ (0.0625) = 1.25 \ \text{gpm} + 1.75 \ \text{gpm} + 0.5 \ \text{gpm} = 3.5 \ \text{gpm}$$

We're well within our flow parameters here, with less worry about friction-related pressure loss because our total runs in ½-in. poly hose are shorter.

Note that we have an overabundance of flow for both Section 2 and Section 3. If we reduced our flow rate for those stations, we would also reduce our pressure loss due to friction. Higher flows through smaller spaces mean greater turbulence and more friction. In fact, microspray works better at lower flow rates because there's less pressure loss due to friction.

Reducing pressure isn't a problem in this scenario. Both the lengths of the pipes and the number of heads can be used to balance out pressure and flow.

Accepting Imperfection

You may have noticed that, even in that somewhat idealized landscape area, coverage was not perfect. There was a slight gap in coverage on the west side, and slight overthrows on the south side. The fact of the matter is that although sectioning can help you regularize much of an irregular figure, the more complex and irregular a figure is, the more difficult it is to fill using simple regular figures.

Sprinkler manufacturers try to help us out by providing a bewildering array of angles (112½°, 135°, and 157½°, just to name a few) but the bottom line is that although you can use regular figures to overfill or underfill an irregular space, it eventually becomes impossible to fill that space exactly.

The problem of filling irregular areas in irrigation design thus becomes a variant of the classic conundrum known as the "coastline of Britain" problem. The smaller the unit you use to measure the coastline of Britain, the longer the coastline becomes, so that as your unit of measure becomes infinitesimally small, the length of the coastline approaches infinity. This is because the coastline of Britain is not a perfectly regular geometric figure.

In the real, irregular world, the irrigation designer must finally be content with close approximation rather than absolute precision. The more complex the landscape, the more approximate its ultimate coverage.

It is for this reason that, from the start of the irrigation project, you should let the coverage patterns provided by the spray heads help determine the placement of the pipe laterals off the main lines. That's why it's wise to section up your landscape mentally, designate areas to be watered, and assign control valves and stations, before you dig your first

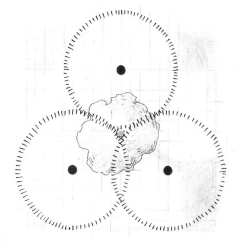

Coverage around Large Trees and Other Obstacles: Triangular Pattern with 360° Heads

Key
● 360° head |||| arc of spray
All heads have a 6-ft. throw radius.

shovelful of dirt or cut your first piece of pipe.

PREVENTING "RAIN SHADOW"

"Rain shadow" provides an opportunity for us to plan irrigation as efficiently as possible, while accepting imperfection. The plans in the drawings on the facing page and this page show the best ways to avoid the dry spots caused by trees. In a complex landscape, it's impossible to avoid some rain shadowing, which is yet another reason for the seeming redundancy of coverage seen in head-to-head spacing—no space is left completely dry.

Coverage around Large Trees and Other Obstacles: Triangular Pattern with 180° Heads

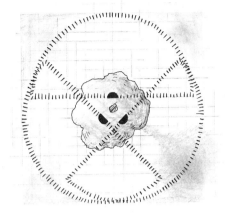

Key

▶ 180° head |||| arc of spray

All heads have a 9-ft. throw radius.

A Parts Checklist

Given the unique characteristics of each landscape, we would be foolish to attempt to create anything like a universal parts list for irrigation systems. However, there is a standard checklist that you should run down for each line coming off a given control valve. When buying parts, take a moment to answer the following questions:

End-distribution units:
• How many do I need on this particular line from this particular control valve?
• What kind (drippers, pop-ups, microspray assemblies, lengths of soaker hose)?

Fittings:
• How many do I need to connect each head to its closest water source?
• What size?
• What kind (pipe nipples for subsurface risers, Marlex street ells and nipples for swing joints, bushings, adapters, compression fittings, distribution tubing and barbs for microspray and bubbler units)?

Couplers:
• How many do I need to get from the manifold to the end-distribution unit?
• What size (1 in., ¾ in., or ½ in. diameter)?
• What kind (tees, crosses, elbows, bushings, adapters, compression fittings)?

• How many at each junction?

Pipe:
• How much do I need to get from the outflow at the control valve on the manifold to the end-distribution units?
• What size (1 in., ¾ in, or ½ in. diameter)?
• What kind (PVC, galvanized, poly hose)?
• What length?

Use this checklist as the skeleton for any parts list you create. If you think it through and fill it out thoroughly, the list can help you avoid a lot of frustrating delays and last-minute trips to the parts store.

Irrigation and the Environment: Final Thoughts

The chart below shows pressure loss through water meters. The end of the book may seem like an odd place to put such information, but we've included it to remind you that water is a limited commodity—and that your irrigation system is part of a larger world.

Most of us know that we live on a planet whose surface is three-quarters covered with water. Far too few of us are aware that the water most important to human beings, and to our crops and animals—fresh water—constitutes only about 2% of all the water on Earth. Even 2% of

Pressure Loss through Water Meters

AWWA Standard/Pressure Loss-PSI

Flow gpm	NOMINAL SIZE					
	⅝ in.	¾ in.	1 in.	1½ in.	2 in.	3 in.
1	0.2	0.1				
2	0.3	0.2				
3	0.4	0.3				
4	0.6	0.5	0.1			
5	0.9	0.6	0.2			
6	1.3	0.7	0.3			
7	1.8	0.8	0.4			
8	2.3	1.0	0.5			
9	3.0	1.3	0.6			
10	3.7	1.6	0.7			
11	4.4	1.9	0.8			
12	5.1	2.2	0.9			
13	6.1	2.6	1.0			
14	7.2	3.1	1.1			
15	8.3	3.6	1.2			
16	9.4	4.1	1.4	0.4		
17	10.7	4.6	1.6	0.5		
18	12.0	5.2	1.8	0.6		
19	13.4	5.8	2.0	0.7		
20	15.0	6.5	2.2	0.8		
22		7.9	2.8	1.0		
24		9.5	3.4	1.2		
26		11.2	4.0	1.4		
28		13.0	4.6	1.6		
30		15.0	5.3	1.8	0.7	
32			6.0	2.1	0.8	
34			6.9	2.4	0.9	
36			7.8	2.7	1.0	
38			8.7	3.0	1.2	
40			9.6	3.3	1.3	
42			10.6	3.6	1.4	
44			11.7	3.9	1.5	
46			12.8	4.2	1.6	
48			13.9	4.5	1.7	
50			15.0	4.9	1.9	0.7
52				5.3	2.1	
54				5.7	2.2	
56				6.2	2.3	

an enormous volume seems like quite a lot, enough to trick us into believing that there will be fresh water for everyone forever.

That is a delusion. The pollution and diminution of fresh water sources is already taking its toll. In the future, potable fresh water is likely to become an increasingly scarce commodity. Runoff from home and field irrigation pollutes streams, rivers, and lakes. Much of that runoff can be avoided. That's why, throughout this book, we have emphasized the link between practical irrigation and efficient water use.

Why hasn't there been a stronger push for more efficient water use? Mainly because governments and utilities around the world have subsidized water distribution by building dams, reservoirs, aqueducts, and canals, leading people in many areas to believe that water is limitlessly plentiful.

We have seen this attitude in action. Stu lives in Palm Springs and has worked in turf and grounds management. He's seen the waste on golf courses and at artificial lakes built in the middle of desert real estate. Howard lives in California's agribusiness-dominated Central Valley, where taxpayer-subsidized water is delivered at phenomenally low cost to corporate farmers who until recently have had little or no incentive to economize.

In Fresno where Howard lives, the citizenry—long accustomed to water that was "too cheap to meter"—went into convulsions when the city began requiring water meters. The meter law was repealed, and the old flat rate system reinstated. Because Howard's irrigation system is highly efficient, Howard and his wife Laurel paid less under the meter system than under the flat rate system. Subsidized water distribution punished them for having a more efficient irrigation system than their neighbors!

The tide is turning, however. More and more municipalities have begun to look askance at profligate water wasting. More and more property owners are planting native or drought-tolerant species. Efficient water use is the wave of the future, but the information and technologies are available today. It is in all our best interests to catch that wave early and ride it for as long and as far as we can. Thoughtful, responsible irrigation can help the planet as well as our plants. It can become a key element in restoring lost habitat and ensuring a greener and more sustainable future for all of us.

GLOSSARY

Adhesion The tendency of water to stick to or "wet" other surfaces.

Anti-siphon valve A valve that breaks the tendency of water to siphon or backflow as a result of atmospheric pressure. Irrigation control valves operate this way.

Arc A segment of a curve. In irrigation design, the angular area covered by water from a spray head, usually a fraction of a circle or 360°.

Ball valve An irrigation flow control that works by swiveling a holed ball into and out of the direction of flow.

Basin irrigation A type of water delivery system in which a flat growing space surrounded by low dikes is flooded.

Black spaghetti *See* Distribution tubing.

Bleeder valve A device, usually manual, for releasing pressure. Generally found as a back-up system on automated sprinkler valves.

Border irrigation A type of water delivery system in which the flooded growing area is usually longer than it is wide, the plot has a bit of a slope, and there is no dike at the far end of the plot.

Branching The directing of water flow through conduits and orifices of progressively smaller diameter, as from a tree trunk through the branches to the leaves.

Bushing An adapter that joins pipes of different diameters by being slipped or threaded inside the pipe.

Center-pivot A system utilizing a swing-arm pipeline that is anchored to an upright at the center of the growing space.

Class *See* Schedules.

Clock timer *See* Sprinkler valve controller.

Cohesion The tendency of water to stick to itself.

Compression tee A three-way intersection coupling fitted with gaskets or slanted slip rings that clamp down on pipes.

Control valve *See* Anti-siphon valve.

Coupler, coupling A linkage that joins lengths of pipe and their associated parts. May be threaded or slip.

Cross A four-way intersection coupling.

Cycling Running through or completing a sequence of activity.

Distribution tubing The generic name for polyethylene line, usually with a diameter of less than ½ in. Poly hose of small diameter often used with microspray and drip systems.

Drain plug *See* Purge valve.

Drip A low-pressure, slow-flow, spot-flooding irrigation method that trickles water into a particular landscape location, often from ½-in. poly hose or ⅛-in. distribution tubing.

Drought-intolerant Plantings accustomed to flourishing in places that do not experience drought during the growing season.

Drought-tolerant Plantings adapted to survive fairly infrequent periods of dry weather.

Ell A two-orifice coupling, bent so that the orifices are at 90° angles to each other. Also called an elbow.

Evapotranspiration The sun-powered movement of water out of plants and into the atmosphere. Also, the total loss of water from soil, including evaporation and plant transpiration.

Female pipe thread (fpt) The part of a spiral interlock system that screws over a male-threaded piece.

Field capacity A soil's capacity for holding water. "Held" water that is available for use by the plant.

Flow The quantity of water that moves past a given point over a given period of time, usually measured in this context in gallons per minute (gpm).

Fogger A sprinkler orifice engineered to implode water droplets and produce a very fine spray.

Furrow irrigation A type of water delivery in which water is channeled into numerous small furrows or ditches, also called creases or corrugations.

G-fitting *See* Compression tee.

Gate valve An irrigation flow control that works by raising a plate out of or lowering a plate into the direction of flow.

Head-to-head coverage When the farthest point of spray from any given head reaches the adjacent heads along its spray arc.

Hose bibb A faucet with a nozzle that is bent downward. Usually mounted on an outdoor wall and threaded to link with a garden hose.

Impact head A sprinkler unit driven by the action of water pressure and flow against a weighted, counterbalanced armature and spring-loaded mechanism. Comes in both lawn head and shrub head variants.

Implosion The collapse of a water droplet into mist.

Inlet An opening into a pipe, valve, sprinkler body, or spray nozzle. *See also* Orifice.

Laterals Pipe lengths projecting from the sides of a coupling, such as from the outflow sides of an elbow, tee, or cross.

Lateral move A type of water delivery system characterized by large diameter wheels spaced at intervals along a central pipe axle. Often an engine is mounted to the pipe structure.

Lawn head A sprinkler unit. The body sits below ground level and a lifter "pops up" or deploys above grass when the unit is in operation.

Lifter A pipe or tube that provides vertical distance between a sprinkler body and a deployed spray nozzle. *See also* Riser.

Lofting When water is propelled in a high arc, often as droplets or mist.

Low Energy Precision Application (LEPA) A type of central-pivot delivery system that supplies water beneath the leaves of the crop, often on long vertical pipe or dangling hose units.

Manifold In irrigation, a structure made of pipes and valves that turns one inflow pipe into multiple, controlled outflow pipes.

Male pipe thread (mpt) The part of a spiral interlock system that screws into a female-threaded orifice.

Matrix Situation or surrounding matter.

Microspray A short-throw sprinkler unit, usually of plastic and consisting of a spike, riser, and spray orifice, connected to small-diameter distribution tubing.

Mister *See* Fogger.

Nipple A short section of pipe that provides distance between adjacent horizontal or vertical pipeline elements, as between tees in a valve manifold or between a sprinkler body and an elbow at the terminus of an underground pipeline. *See also* Riser.

Nozzle An opening at the end of a hose or pipeline through which a spray or stream of water is discharged.

Orifice An opening into or out of a pipe, valve, sprinkler body, or spray nozzle. *See also* Inlet; Outlet.

Outlet The opening out of a pipe, valve, sprinkler body, or spray nozzle. *See also* Orifice.

Poly hose Flexible, ultraviolet-resistant polyethylene tubing, most commonly used in ½-in. diameter, running at or near the surface of the ground.

Pop-up *See* Lawn head.

Pressure The amount of force applied over a surface, measured as force per unit of area. In this context, usually described in pounds per square inch (psi).

Purge valve A device that allows water to drain out of a pipe when the water pressure falls below a preset value. Also called drain plugs.

PVC Polyvinyl chloride. Irrigation's "white pipes" are made of this ultraviolet-sensitive, fairly rigid plastic.

Ramification The process of branching out or dividing and developing into branches.

Reducer A coupling that decreases the diameter of an orifice or conduit, as in a ¾-in.-to-½-in. bell reducer, which steps down the flow diameter from ¾ in. to ½ in. Inverted, a reducer can also be used to increase diameter.

Retrofit The renovation of an established irrigation system or an established landscape, or both.

Riser A pipe or tube that provides vertical distance between an inlet and an outlet, as between a pipeline and a sprinkler body, between a sprinkler body and a deployed spray nozzle, or between the spike and the spray outlet of a microspray unit. *See also* Lifter.

Runoff Precipitation not absorbed by the soil.

Schedules Gradations of PVC pipe, classified by wall thickness. The higher the schedule number, the thinner the wall of the pipe.

Sectioning, sectorializing Regularizing the mixed geometry of a landscape by dividing the landscape into regular geo-metric forms.

Shrub head A sprinkler unit that stands permanently above ground and does not pop up.

Slip Unthreaded or smooth, often referring to pipe fittings.

Soaker hose A highly porous tube of variable length that leaks water onto and into the soil surface.

Sola Surface layers of soil profiles, in which topsoil formation occurs.

Solenoid An electromagnetic device that controls the flow of water through the valve and pipes.

Spike The plastic base of a microspray unit, which is jammed into the soil and holds the microspray unit upright.

Spray head The nozzle, stream, or spray orifice of a sprinkler unit.

Sprinkler unit The body, internal mechanism, and nozzle of a sprinkler.

Sprinkler valve controller A timing mechanism that actively tells your irrigation system when, how long, and how often to water, as well as which pipelines and spray heads to use.

Square spacing A method of head-to-head spray coverage for a given landscape, based on dividing the landscape into squares.

Station The switching assembly in the controller that governs the activation and deactivation of a single control valve in the manifold, as well as the flow of water through the pipes and spray units associated with that valve.

Stream rotor A gear-driven sprinkler head mechanism that covers a given arc and throw radius by the application of a rotating stream or streams of water. Comes in both lawn head and shrub head variants.

Street ells Elbow fittings made of black Marlex plastic, charac-terized by male threading on one end and female threading on the other.

Swing joint A structure made of Marlex street ells and a nipple, which together provide flexibility along virtually all axes of rotation.

Tee A three-way intersection coupling, shaped like the capital letter T.

Tensiometer A torsion-balance apparatus used to measure the surface tension of a liquid.

Throw, throw distance, throw radius The distance that pressure and flow propel water droplets from a spray orifice. The distance from the sprinkler head to the point where the farthest water droplets hit the ground.

Tilth Tilled earth.

Time clock *See* Sprinkler valve controller.

Triangular spacing A method of spray-covering a given landscape area, based on dividing spaces into triangles. Provides less complete coverage than square spacing.

Water gun A unit with a large throw radius, requiring high pressure and flow. Usually of the single-stream rotor variety. Used in estate, athletic field, golf course, and agricultural applications.

Xeriscape Refers to landscape plantings that even in dry climates require little or no added watering beyond that supplied by nature.

Zone A landscape area watered by a single station on a sprinkler valve controller.

SOURCES OF SUPPLY

It practically goes without saying that large chains such as Home Depot and Orchard Supply Hardware carry most if not all of the materials you're likely to need to build a landscape irrigation system. We've also found the following companies to be good sources.

Aquapore Moisture Systems
610 South 80th Ave.
Phoenix, AZ 85043
(602) 936-8083
Soaker hose

Fungi Perfecti
P.O. Box 7634
Olympia, WA 98507
(206) 426-9292
Beneficial fungi

James Hardie Irrigation
27361 La Paz Road
Laguna Niguel, CA 92656
(800) 231-5117
Water guns

LASCO Fluid Distribution Products
3255 E. Miraloma Ave.
Anaheim, CA 92806
(714) 961-9755
Fittings and couplers

NIBCO Irrigation Systems
2851 E. Florence Ave.
Fresno, CA 93721
(800) 695-7171
Microspray and spaghetti line

Orbit Sprinklers
Bountiful, UT 84010
(801) 299-5555
Stationary shrub and pop-up heads

The Toro Company
Irrigation Division
P.O. Box 489
Riverside, CA 92502
(800) 654-1882
A wide range of products, including single- and multiple-stream rotors

INDEX

Book Publisher: Jim Childs

Acquisitions Editor: Helen Albert

Editorial Assistant: Cherilyn DeVries

Editor: Ruth Hamel

Designer: Lynne Phillips

Layout Artist: Thomas Lawton, Rosalie Vaccaro

Illustrator: Christopher Clapp

Photographer: Mike Chen

Typeface: Stone serif

Paper: 70-lb. Moistrite Matte

Printer: Quebecor Printing/Hawkins, Church Hill, Tennessee